Alexander Jones • Joachim Klang

TIPS FOR KIDS

TRANSFORMER

COOL PROJECTS FOR YOUR LEGO® BRICKS

HEEL

THANKS

To pioneers and revolutionaries, some of whom we know personally and admire:

2LegoOrNot2Lego	- Derfel Cadarn -	Karwik	McBricker	Spencer_R
Arvo Brothers	Digger1221	Lazer Blade	Mijasper	T.Oechsner
ArzLan	Eastpole77	lego_nabii	Misterzumbi	Taz-Maniac
Bart Willen	Fianat	Legohaulic	Nannan Z	ted @ndes
Brian Corredor	Fraslund	LEGOLAS	NENN	TheBrickAvenger
Bricksonwheels	Fredoichi	Legonardo Davidy	Obedient Machine	Théolego
Brickthing	Gabe Umland	Legopard	Ochre Jelly	tnickolaus
Bricktrix	Gambort	Legotrucks	„Orion Pax"	Toltomeja
Bruceywan	gearcs	_lichtblau_	Paul Vermeesch	x_Speed
captainsmog	Henrik Hoexbroe	‚LL'	Pepa Quin	Xenomurphy
Cole Blaq	Homa	Mark of Falworth	RoccoB	
Cuahchic	Joe Meno	markus19840420	Sir Nadroj	
DecoJim	Jojo	marshal banana	Sirens-Of-Titan	

Particular thanks to Lutz Uhlmann, als always, for digitizing our constructions. To Niko Chief Togusa for his long lasting friendship. And special thanks, of course, to our wives for their permanent support and understanding.

HEEL Verlag GmbH
Gut Pottscheidt
53639 Königswinter
Germany
Tel.: +49 (0) 2223 9230-0
Fax: +49 (0) 2223 9230-13
E-Mail: info@heel-verlag.de
www.heel-verlag.de

© 2017 HEEL Verlag GmbH

Authors: Alexander Jones and Joachim Klang
Layout, Design and Illustration: Odenthal Illustration, www.odenthal-illustration.de
Photography: Thomas Schultze, www.thomas-schultze.de
Translated from German by: Laila Friese in association with First Edition Translations Ltd, Cambridge, UK
Edited by: Robert Anderson in association with First Edition Translations Ltd, Cambridge, UK
Project management: Ulrike Reihn-Hamburger

Printed in Hungary

ISBN 978-3-95843-495-0

CONTENT

58

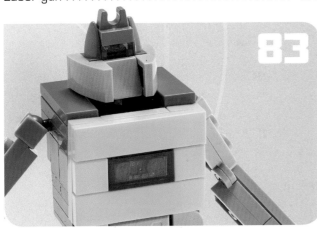

83

130

97

FOREWORD

I bet there is hardly anyone who has never heard of Transformers. They are a part of popular culture, like Star Wars, Star Trek, or Masters of the Universe. They first appeared in a cartoon series in the 1980s. These transformable action figures are as fascinating as ever and have even been the main protagonists in Hollywood films.

Models that can change into something else? That makes me think of LEGO® right away. I've always said you can make anything from these extraordinary bricks.

When I started planning this book I immediately got hold of Alexander Jones, also known as Orion Pax. For as long as I've known him, he has come up with one amazing Transformers model after another. As soon as LEGO® comes out with new bricks, he rebuilds everything and is always on the lookout for the next optimum solution, especially for his model of Optimus Prime.

Of course, I would love to design these models myself but, as they say, "Why reinvent the wheel?" I just assumed that Alex had already thought through all the possible solutions and tried them out, which makes him the expert on this topic, as far as I am concerned. Well, so I just telephoned him then and there and "tadaa"—here's the result!

Of course, I couldn't just sit around and watch while someone made models with LEGO® bricks. So, in some of the photos you'll also see something I have built, but Alex gets the credit for all the main models.

Transformers models made out of LEGO® are nothing new, but what's so special about Alex's models is that they are transformable! With a few deft hand movements, they transform from a truck, a beetle, or a radio recorder into a robot. Since this is a book, we can't play you a video that shows the transformations, so we decided to opt for photos. With some practice, I'm sure you'll quickly be able to see the transformations you can make with the models.

The larger the model, the more difficult it is for it to be robust and playable with. That's why we decided to compromise and show you different sizes: a small Optimus Prime, which is really easy to build and play with, as well as a more imposing large model, which is a bit more fragile and probably more suitable for the shelf or the display case, but transformable!

Since Alex "Orion Pax" Jones is a total Transformers fan, he has built more and more models over the years—more than what we can include in this book with building instructions. In the photos you'll therefore see some additional models, which will hopefully inspire you. Building models only according to instructions can get boring after a while, after all.

We're all creative! Just put some bricks together and see where it takes you. That's how we all get started. Enjoy!

INTRODUCTION

As a child of the 1980s I grew up with cable television. On Sky Channel's weekend morning children's show they broadcast Fun Factory, which showed a lot of cartoons. One of these was The Transformers, which was among the most successful of the time. I was fascinated by the series and I got up extra early at the weekends to make sure I didn't miss a single episode. The concept, a common one at the time, was to advertise a toy using a cartoon series. Children could identify themselves with the heroes in the series and then build a stronger relationship with the products on the toy-store shelves. The Transformers' slogan was "Robots in Disguise".

As a child, I never had as many Transformers toys as some of my friends, but I often got LEGO® for my birthday or Christmas. So the next logical step was to design my own models. I built my first spaceships from movies like Star Wars with my uncle's help. Transformers, however, were really difficult to build. I kept making versions of Optimus Prime but never managed one that could transform.

The inspiration to build Transformers from LEGO® may have started in childhood, but I still have the bug. And the colors and shapes that LEGO® produces fit the Transformers' design language really well. Functional parts, such as the MIXEL Ball Joints, which have appeared in recent years, make it possible to have stable transformation steps and to get the alignment right for the figures in robot form.

Over the past twelve years, I've had many new ideas and have collected many different designs. In this book I'd like to show you some of these in detail, give you explanations and instructions, and show you tips and tricks on how to build your own Transformers.

As Optimus Prime always says, "May the Matrix light our darkest hour!"

OK, then—lights on and off to Cybertron!

ALEX "ORIONPAX" Jong

ALEX "ORIONPAX" Jong

You can see really clearly here how the vehicles all go together. Most of the vehicles are built 8 studs wide to make sure there's enough room to manage the transformation steps.

GLOSSARY

Here are some specialist terms from the world of the Transformers with some explanations:

Cybertron:	A planet made of metal—home of the Autobots and Decepticons
Autobots:	Workers on Cybertron who fight for good
Decepticons:	Warriors on Cybertron who fight for evil
Ark:	The Autobots' spaceship
Nemesis:	The Decepticons' spaceship
Matrix of Leadership:	An artifact belonging to the Autobots, worn by their leader
Altmode:	Alternative shape
Botmode:	Robot shape
Mount St. Hilary:	The place on Earth (in Oregon) where the Ark crashed and which became the headquarters of the Autobots
Energon:	Source of energy in the form of cubes made from Earth's raw materials
Teletraan I:	The Autobots' main computer in the Ark's control room
Optimus Prime:	Leader of the Autobots
Megatron:	Leader of the Decepticons
Combiner:	When several Transformers make up one robot

ARK

More than 4 million years ago, on the planet Cybertron, the Autobots and the Decepticons fought a battle for the planet's last resources. The Autobots decided to leave the planet to find a new home. They were left stranded by the Decepticons. The Ark, the Autobots' spaceship, was their last chance to leave Cybertron. This version in micro scale is very original and a great little model for your collection.

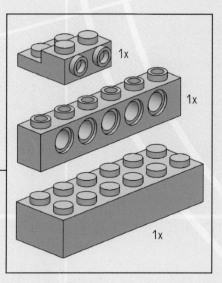

1

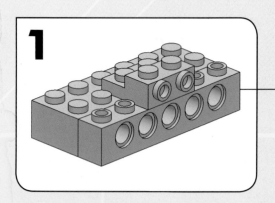

1x

1x

1x

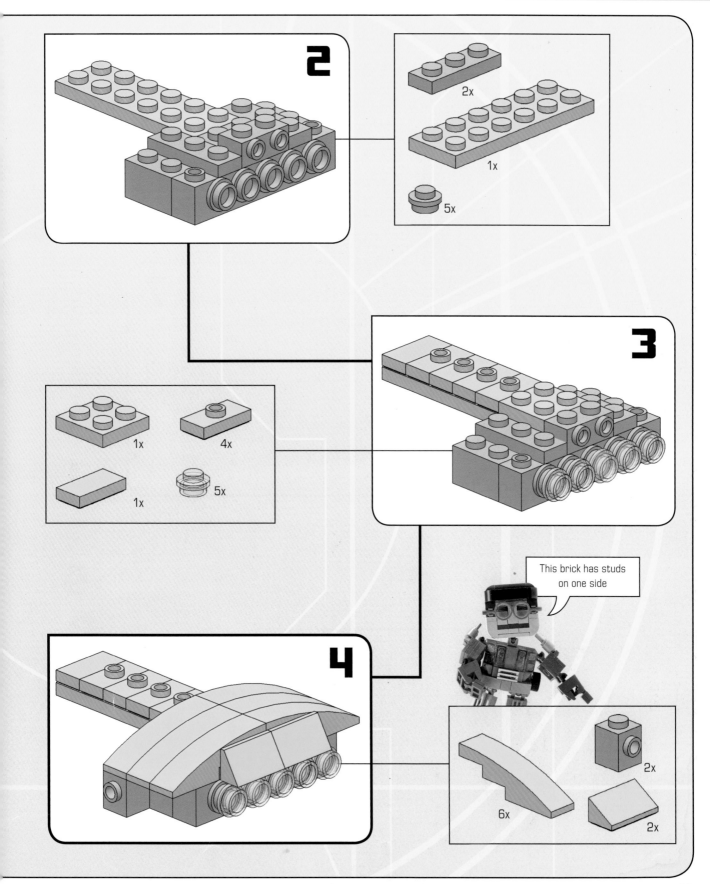

2

2x

1x

5x

3

1x

4x

1x

5x

This brick has studs on one side

4

6x

2x

2x

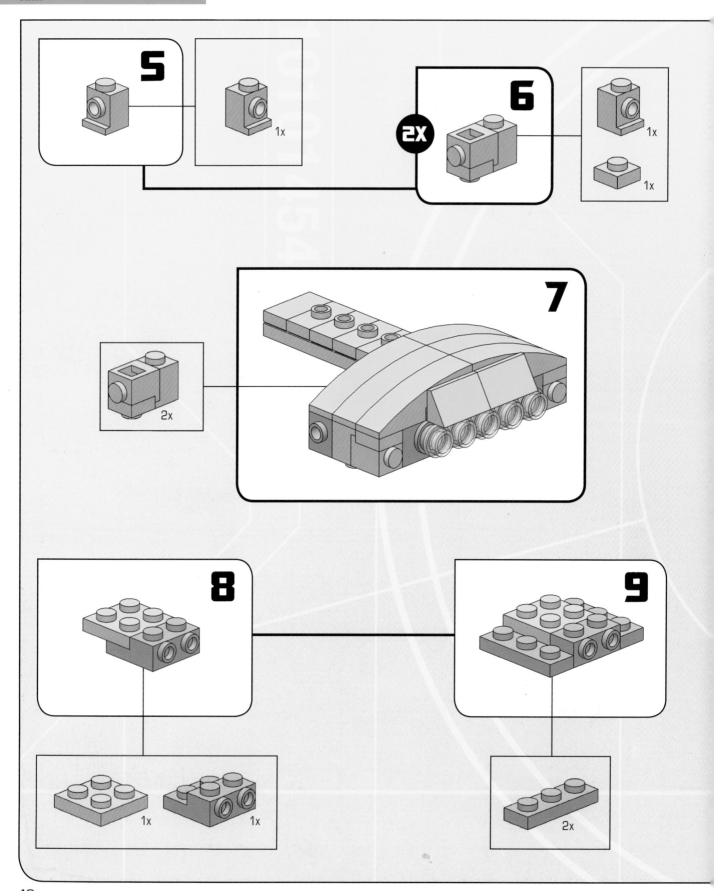

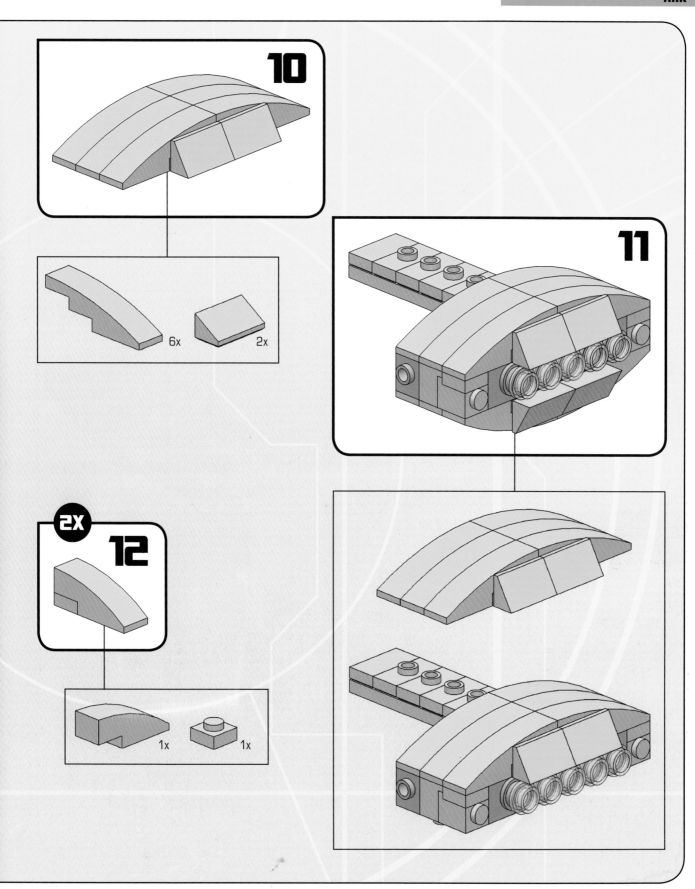

10

6x 2x

11

2x

12

1x 1x

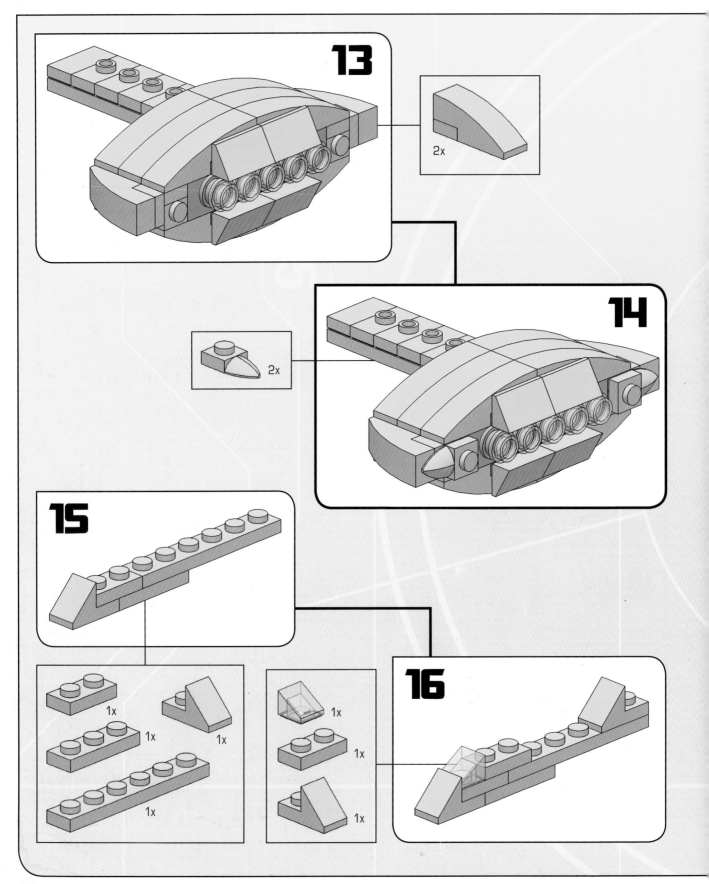

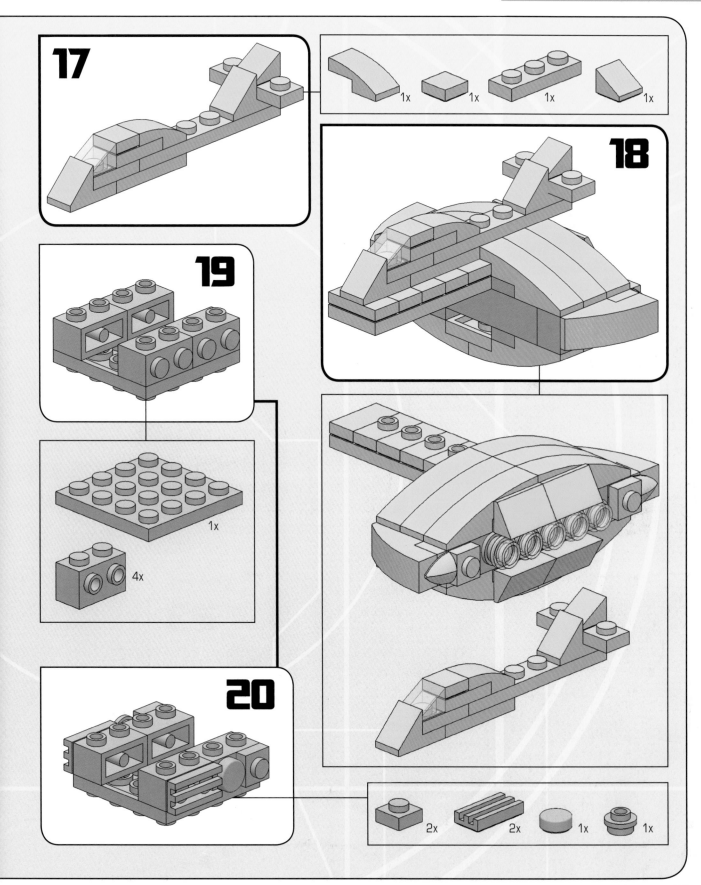

17

1x 1x 1x 1x

18

19

1x

4x

20

2x 2x 1x 1x

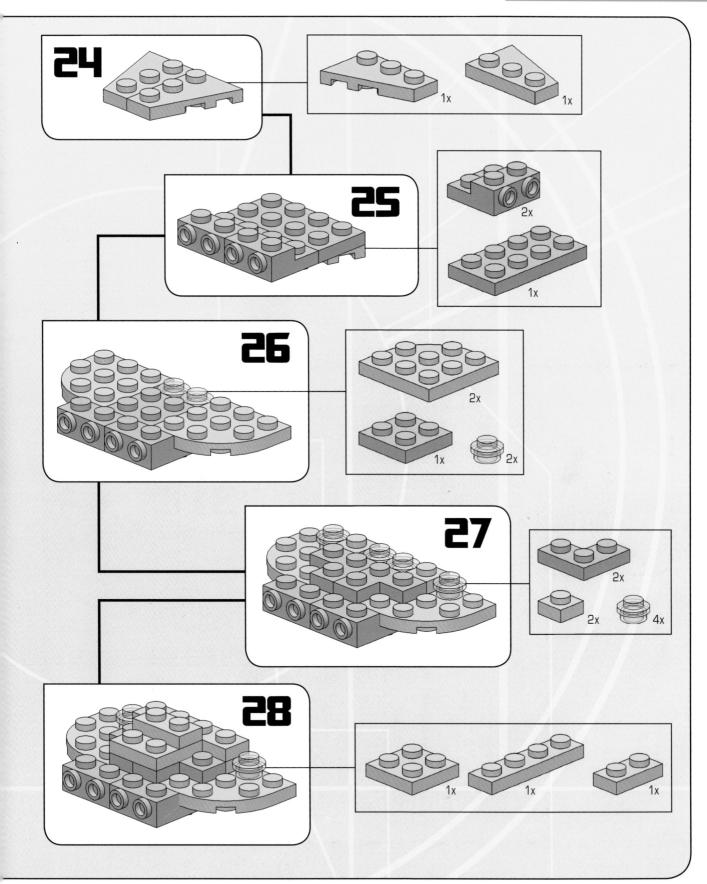

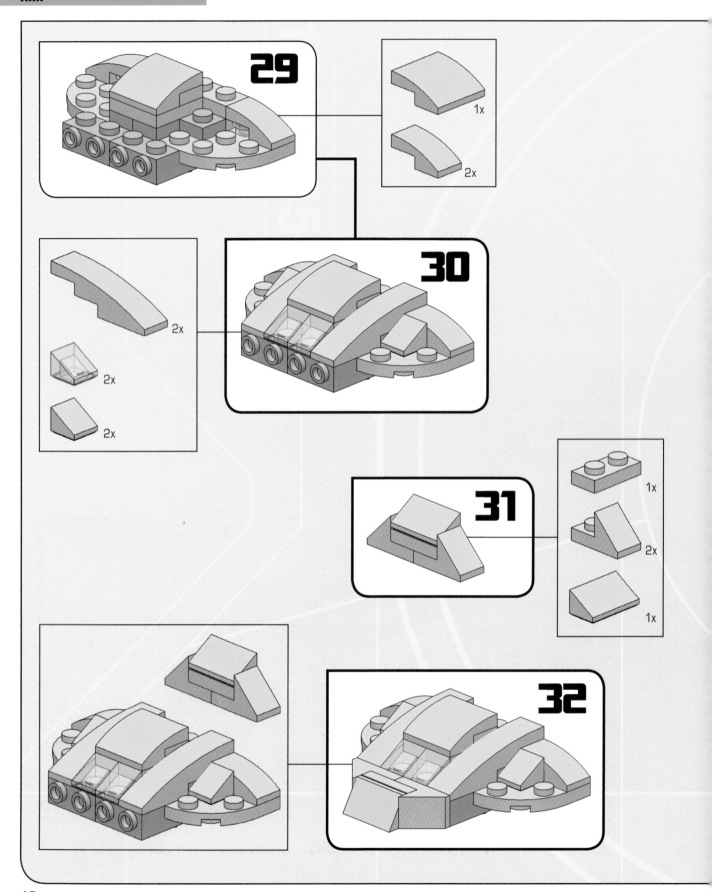

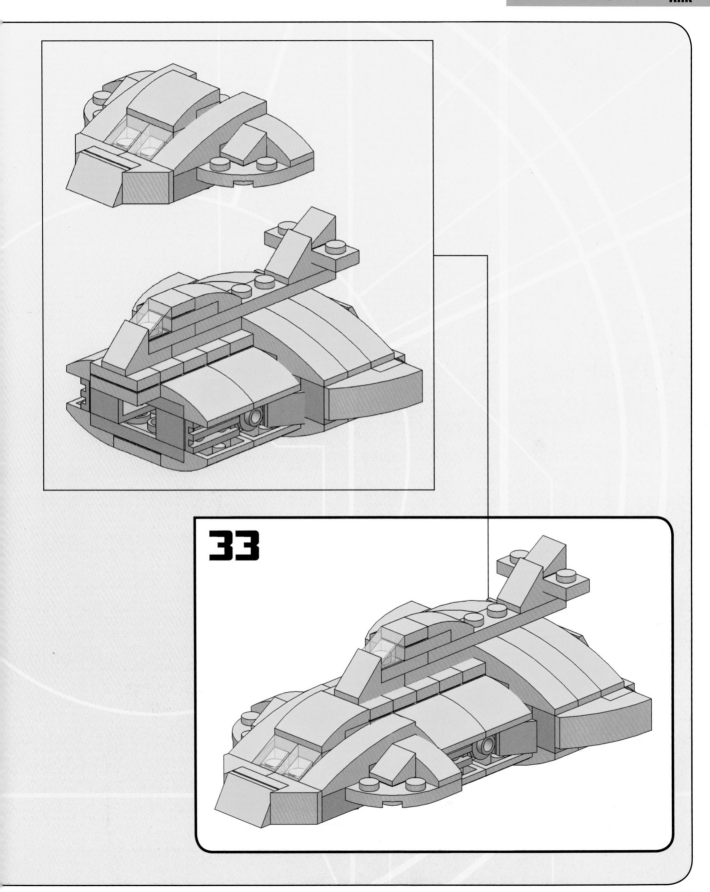

33

PARTS LIST

Quantity		Color	Element	Element Name	LEGO® Number
4		Bright Light Orange	4070	Brick 1 x 1 with Headlight	6020098, 6186006
2		Light Bluish Gray	87087	Brick 1 x 1 with Stud on 1 Side	4558953
4		Light Bluish Gray	52107	Brick 1 x 2 with Studs on Sides	4657459
1		Light Bluish Gray	2456	Brick 2 x 6	4211795
6		Bright Light Orange	3024	Plate 1 x 1	6073040
2		Light Bluish Gray	3024	Plate 1 x 1	4211399
5		Light Bluish Gray	4073	Plate 1 x 1 Round	4211525
11		Trans Light Blue	4073	Plate 1 x 1 Round	4163917
1		Light Bluish Gray	85861	Plate 1 x 1 Round with Open Stud	6124825, 6168647
2		Bright Light Orange	49668	Plate 1 x 1 with Tooth In-line	4282860
4		Bright Light Orange	3023	Plate 1 x 2	6028736
4		Bright Light Orange	3794b	Plate 1 x 2 with Groove with 1 Centre Stud	6122504
2		Bright Light Orange	3623	Plate 1 x 3	6073042
4		Light Bluish Gray	3623	Plate 1 x 3	3623194, 4211429
1		Bright Light Orange	3710	Plate 1 x 4	6020073
1		Bright Light Orange	3666	Plate 1 x 6	6020074
3		Bright Light Orange	3022	Plate 2 x 2	4243776, 6003033
1		Light Bluish Gray	3022	Plate 2 x 2	4211397
2		Light Bluish Gray	2420	Plate 2 x 2 Corner	4211353
4		Light Bluish Gray	99206	Plate 2 x 2 x 0.667 with Two Studs On Side and Two Raised	4654577
1		Light Bluish Gray	3020	Plate 2 x 4	4211395
1		Bright Light Orange	3795	Plate 2 x 6	6097509
2		Bright Light Orange	30357	Plate 3 x 3 Corner Round	6022078
2		Light Bluish Gray	3031	Plate 4 x 4	4211403, 4243797
3		Bright Light Orange	54200	Slope Brick 31 1 x 1 x 0.667	6023173
2		Light Bluish Gray	54200	Slope Brick 31 1 x 1 x 0.667	4521921
3		Trans Light Blue	54200	Slope Brick 31 1 x 1 x 0.667	6073445
5		Bright Light Orange	85984	Slope Brick 31 1 x 2 x 0.667	6024286
3		Bright Light Orange	11477	Slope Brick Curved 2 x 1	6099728
9		Bright Light Orange	15068	Slope Brick Curved 2 x 2 x 0.667	6099730
2		Bright Light Orange	50950	Slope Brick Curved 3 x 1	6022064

Quantity	Color	Element	Element Name	LEGO® Number
14	Bright Light Orange	61678	Slope Brick Curved 4 x 1	6020093, 6045944
4	Bright Light Orange	92946	Slope Plate 45 2 x 1	6020106, 6069171
1	Light Bluish Gray	3894	Technic Brick 1 x 6 with Holes	4211466
1	Light Bluish Gray	98138	Tile 1 x 1 Round with Groove	4650260
1	Bright Light Orange	3070b	Tile 1 x 1 with Groove	6065504
2	Light Bluish Gray	2412b	Tile 1 x 2 Grille with Groove	4211350
3	Bright Light Orange	3069b	Tile 1 x 2 with Groove	4622062
1	Dark Bluish Gray	15535	Tile 2 x 2 Round with Hole	6055313
1	Bright Light Orange	43723	Wing 2 x 3 Left	6020145
1	Bright Light Orange	43722	Wing 2 x 3 Right	6020146

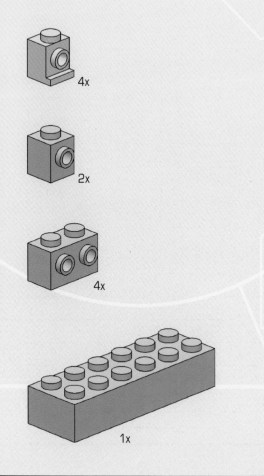

4x

2x

4x

1x

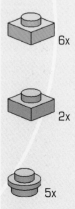

6x

2x

5x

11x

1x

2x

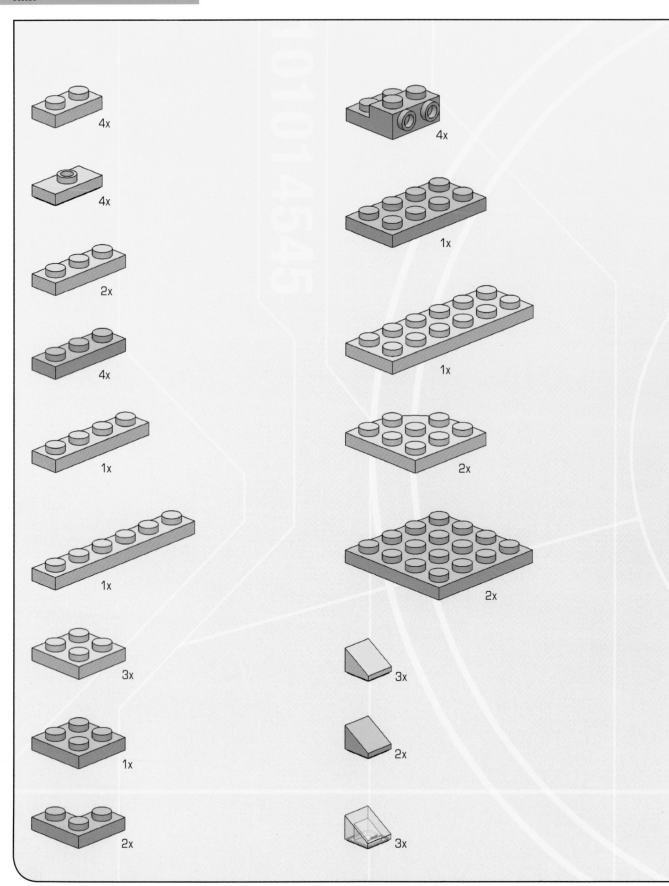

4x

4x

2x

4x

1x

1x

3x

1x

2x

4x

1x

1x

2x

2x

3x

2x

3x

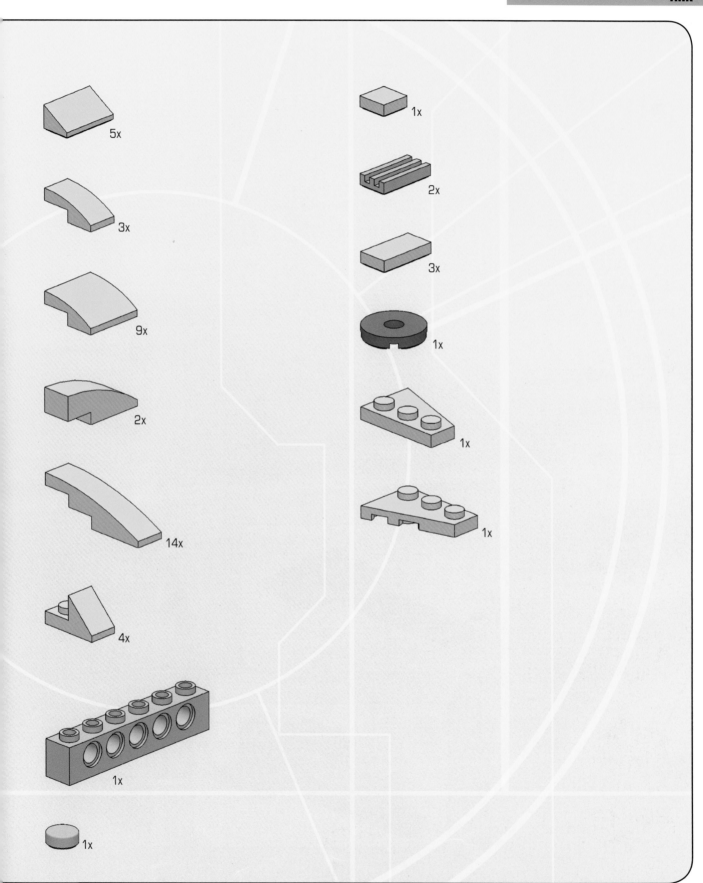

5x

3x

9x

2x

14x

4x

1x

1x

1x

2x

3x

1x

1x

1x

NEMESIS

So like the Autobots' Ark, this spaceship was the Decepticons' last chance to escape their destroyed home planet, Cybertron. The Decepticons pursue the Autobots and then crash on Earth along with them. The models of the two spaceships are great for playing with, but you can also build them onto a small base plate to display on a shelf.

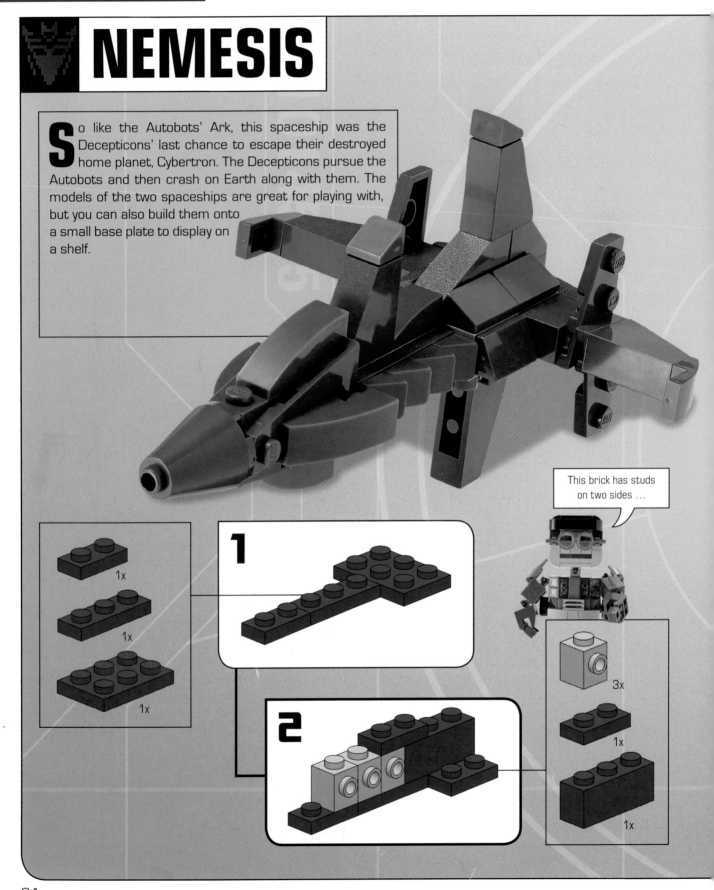

This brick has studs on two sides ...

1

1x

1x

1x

2

3x

1x

1x

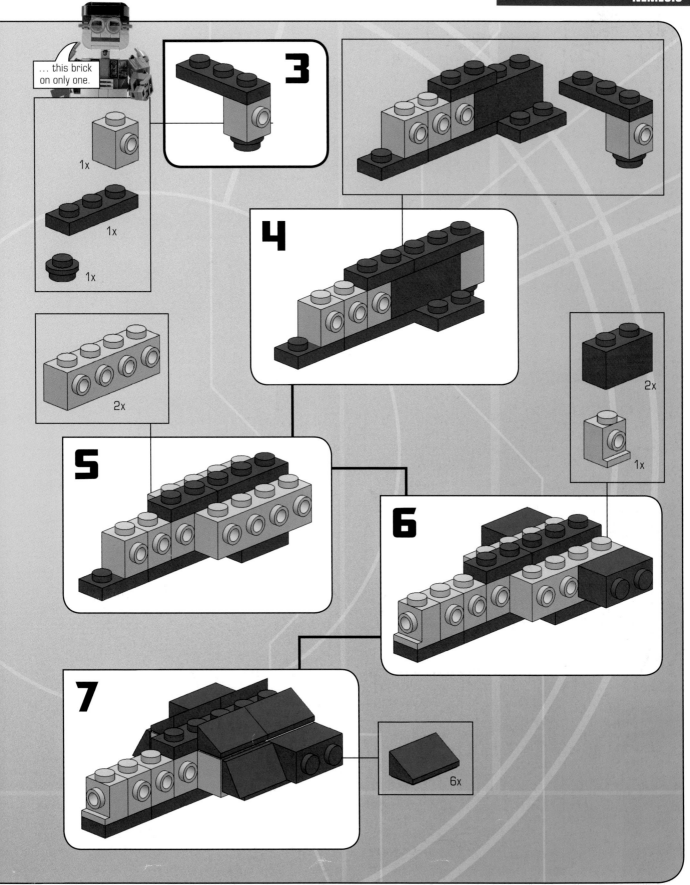

... this brick on only one.

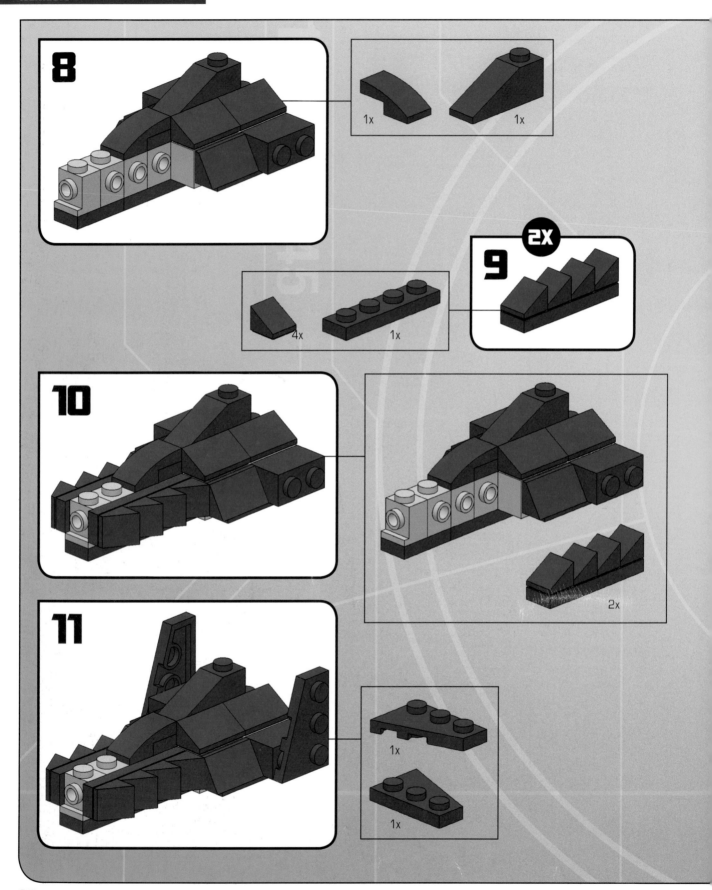

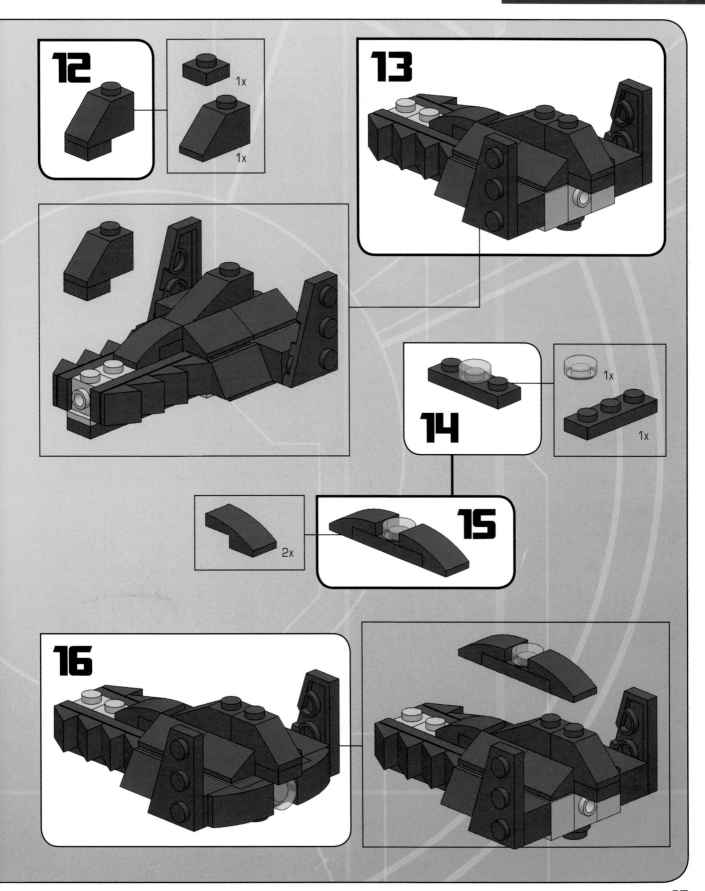

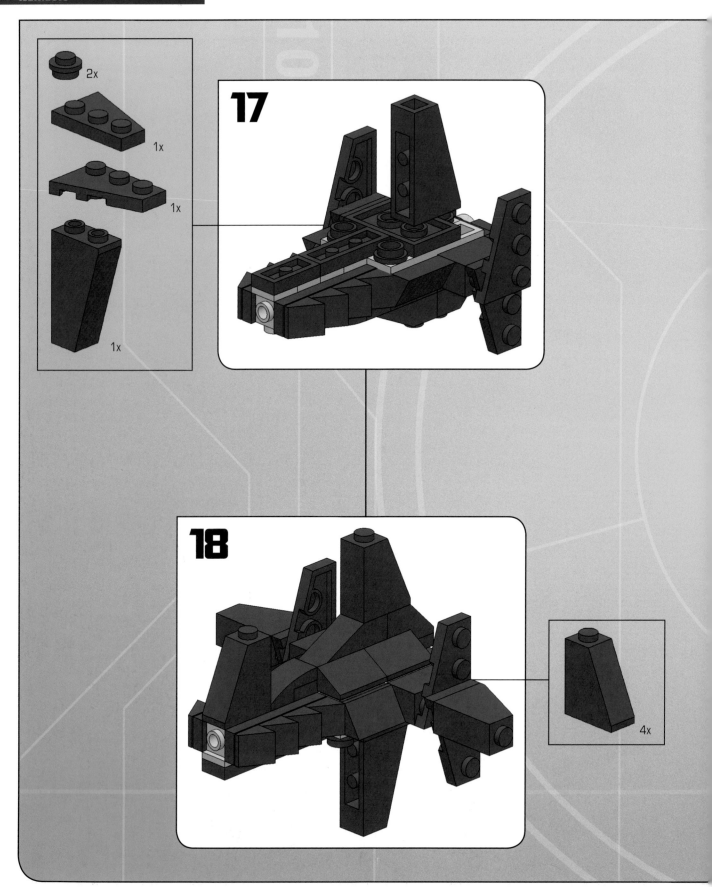

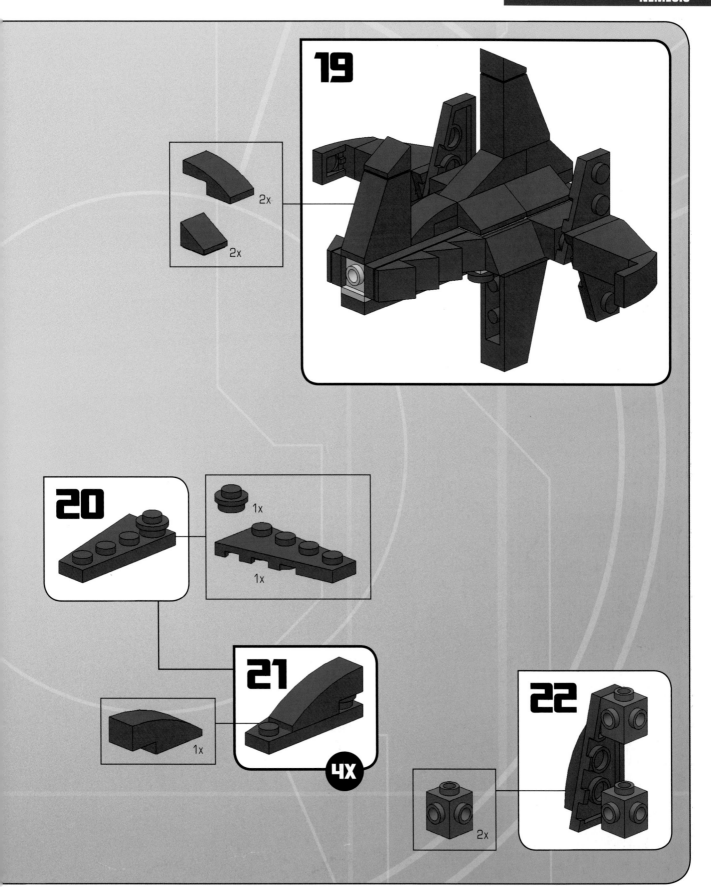

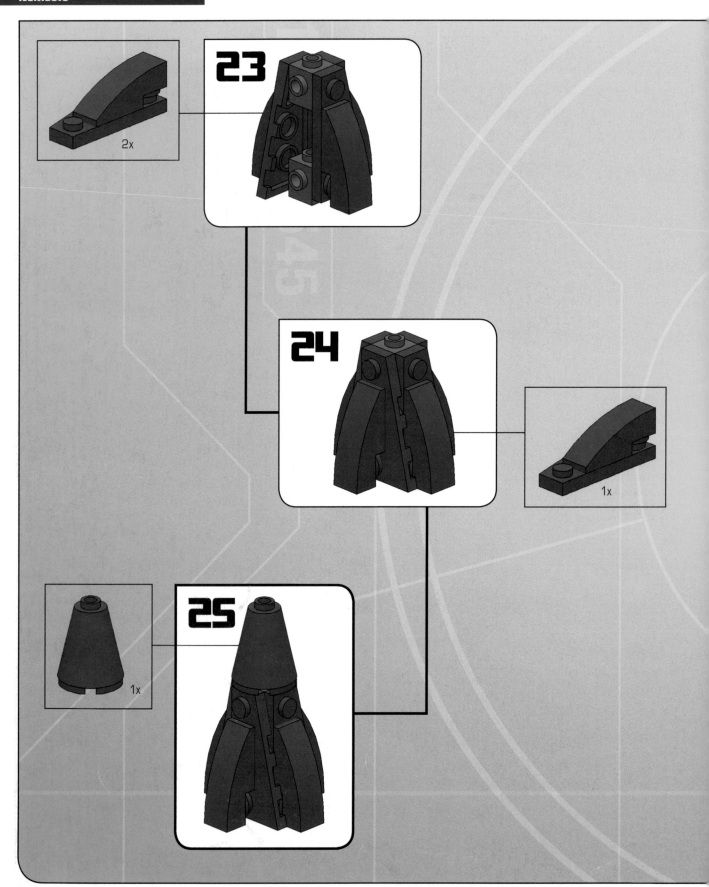

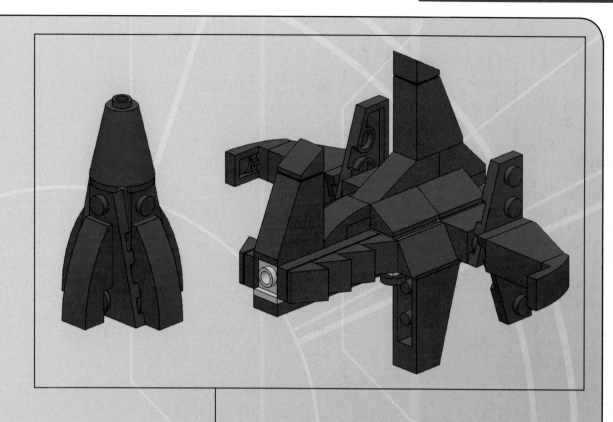

26

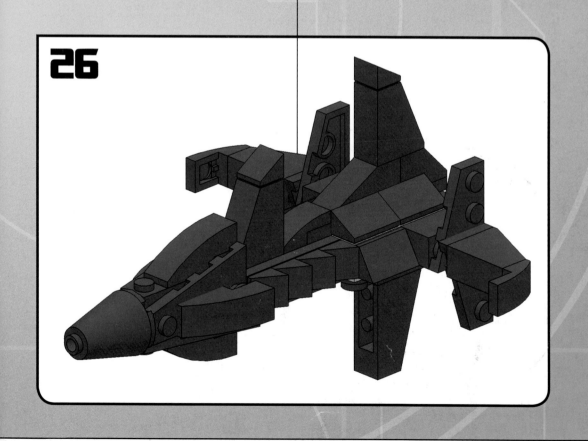

PARTS LIST

Quantity	Color		Element	Element Name	LEGO® Number
1		Light Bluish Gray	4070	Brick 1 x 1 with Headlight	4211476
1		Light Bluish Gray	87087	Brick 1 x 1 with Stud on 1 Side	4558953
2		Blue	4733	Brick 1 x 1 with Studs on Four Sides	4296151
3		Light Bluish Gray	47905	Brick 1 x 1 with Studs on Two Opposite Sides	4213567
2		Dark Purple	3004	Brick 1 x 2	4224854, 4640739, 6104154
1		Dark Purple	3622	Brick 1 x 3	4235127
2		Light Bluish Gray	30414	Brick 1 x 4 with Studs on Side	4211636
1		Dark Purple	3942c	Cone 2 x 2 x 2 with Hollow Stud Open	4297454, 6060830, 6064621
1		Dark Purple	3024	Plate 1 x 1	4224857
7		Dark Purple	4073	Plate 1 x 1 Round	4566522
2		Dark Purple	3023	Plate 1 x 2	4224858, 4655695
3		Dark Purple	3623	Plate 1 x 3	6035470
2		Dark Purple	3710	Plate 1 x 4	4225140, 6167464
1		Dark Purple	3021	Plate 2 x 3	4225142
10		Dark Purple	54200	Slope Brick 31 1 x 1 x 0.667	4255409, 4567509
6		Dark Purple	85984	Slope Brick 31 1 x 2 x 0.667	4566607
1		Dark Purple	4286	Slope Brick 33 3 x 1	4225012, 4567508
1		Dark Purple	3040	Slope Brick 45 2 x 1	4225265, 6109814
4		Dark Purple	60481	Slope Brick 65 2 x 1 x 2	6022070
1		Dark Purple	2449	Slope Brick 75 2 x 1 x 3 Inverted	6022072
5		Dark Purple	11477	Slope Brick Curved 2 x 1	6057390
4		Dark Purple	50950	Slope Brick Curved 3 x 1	4578772, 6103449
1		Trans Purple	98138	Tile 1 x 1 Round with Groove	6065505
2		Dark Purple	43723	Wing 2 x 3 Left	4616558
2		Dark Purple	43722	Wing 2 x 3 Right	4616557
4		Dark Purple	41769	Wing 2 x 4 Right	4225145

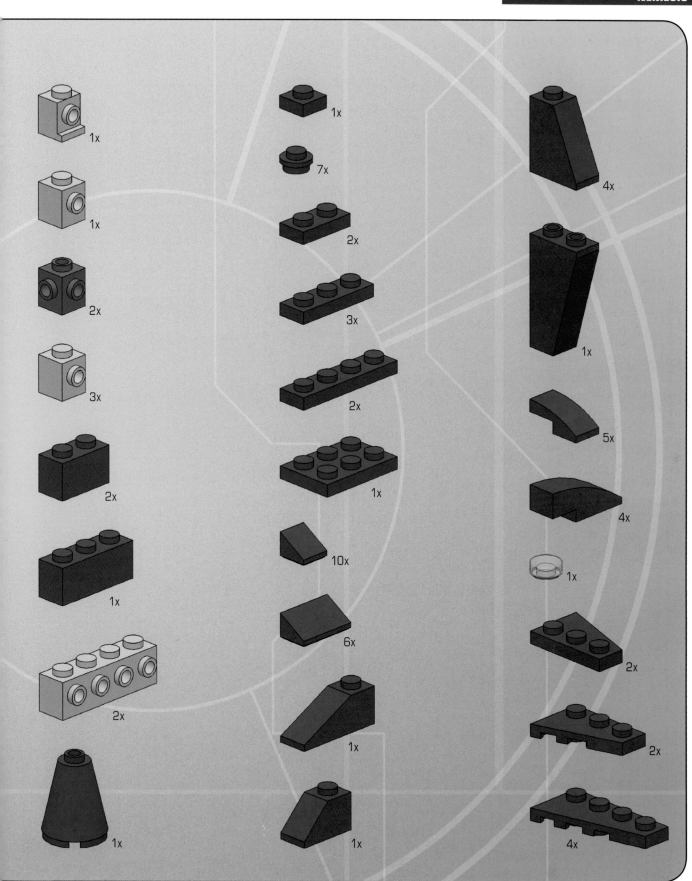

TRANSFORMATION PROBE

This is part of the Teletraan I restart program. After crashing on Earth, the program is activated in order to find suitable shapes in the planet's environment and transfer them to the robots. On Cybertron, the Transformers used the ability to transform only to help them move about; on Earth, it is also used as camouflage.

Of course, the size of the robot and the object into which it is transformed have to match—but this limitation was never taken very seriously in the cartoons.

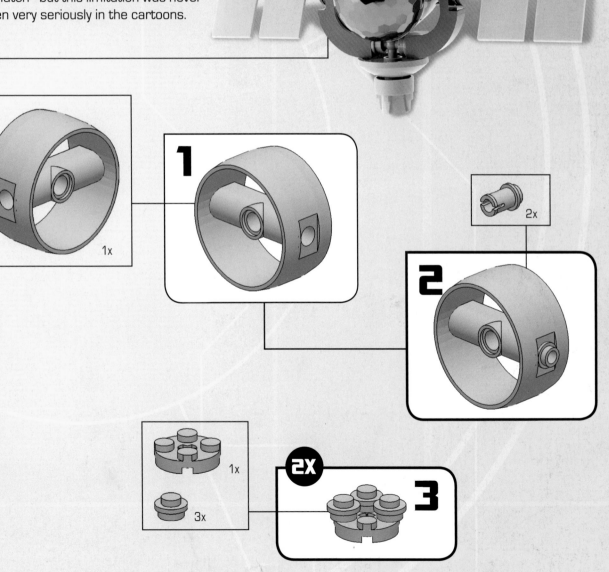

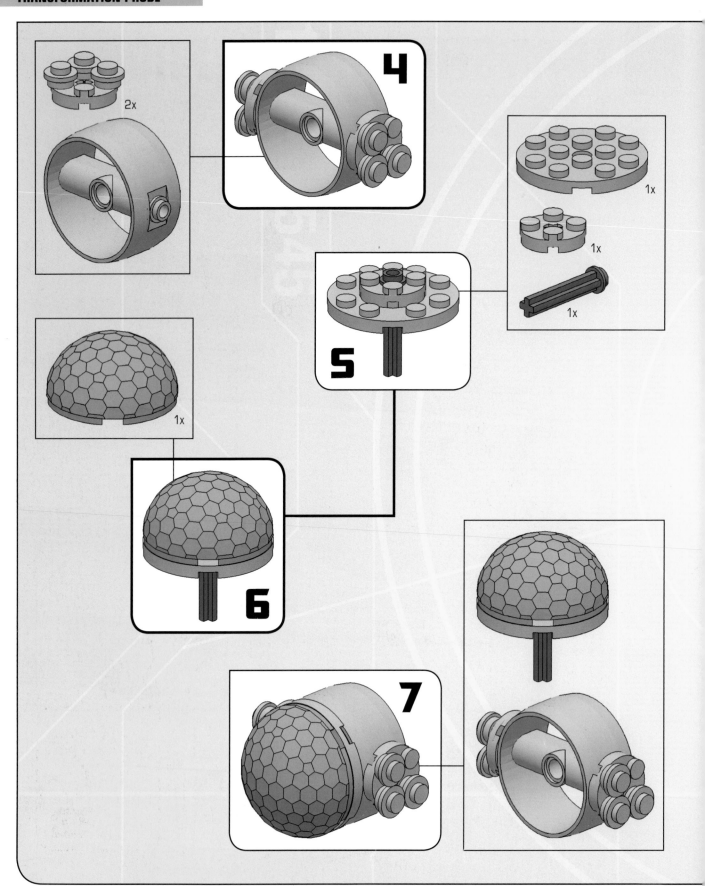

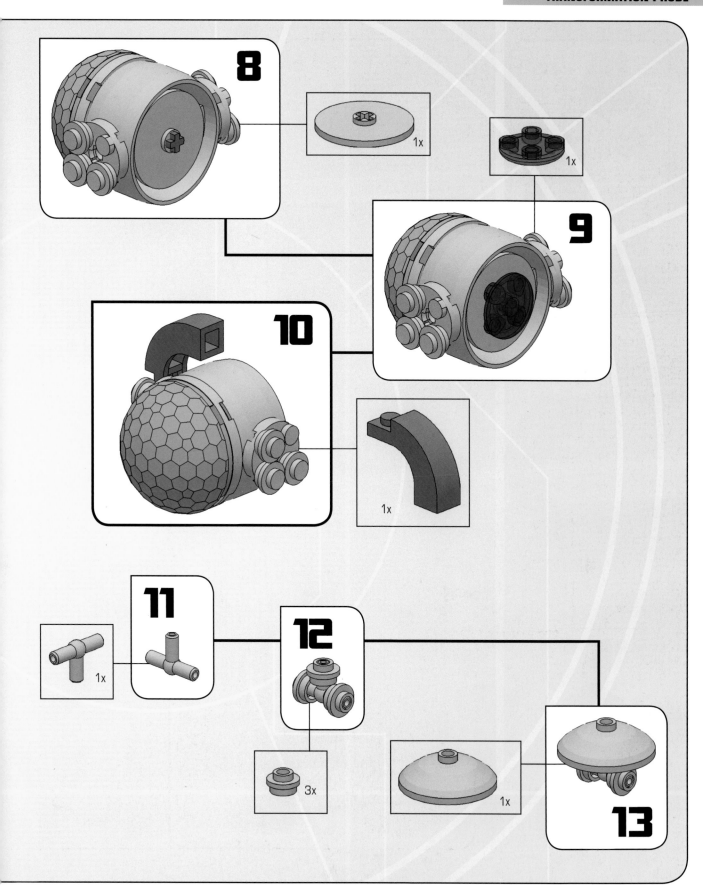

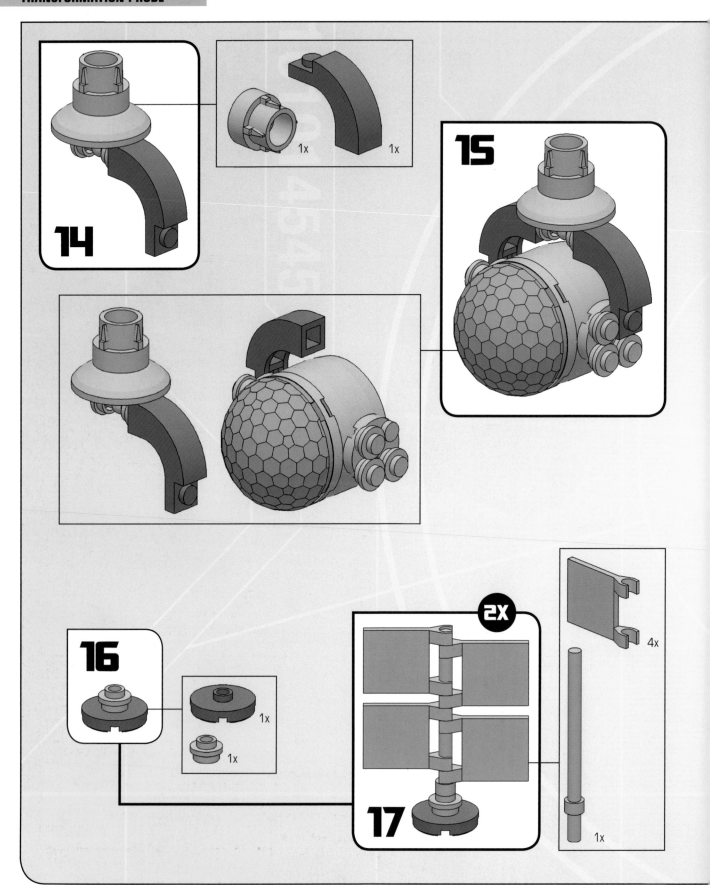

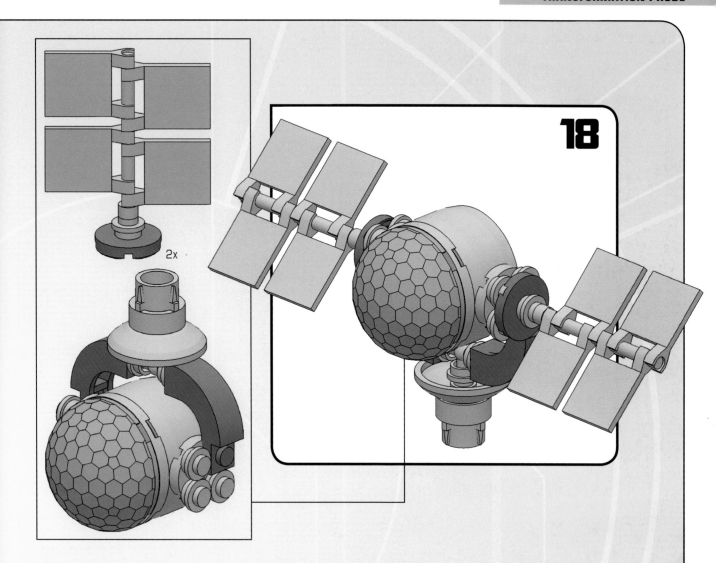

18

2x

PARTS LIST

Quantity	Color		Element	Element Name	LEGO® Number
2		Dark Bluish Gray	6005	Arch 1 x 3 x 2 with Curved Top	4199213, 4586564, 4618881
2		Light Bluish Gray	63965	Bar 6L with Thick Stop	4538098, 6061535, 6081975
1		Trans Dark Blue	2654	Dish 2 x 2	4278413, 4529172, 4623595
1		Light Bluish Gray	43898	Dish 3 x 3 Inverted	4211787, 4568360, 6070564
8		Light Bluish Gray	2335	Flag 2 x 2	4271362, 4523408, 6011817
1		Chrome Blue	30208	Hemisphere 4 x 4 Multifaceted	4295298
6		Light Bluish Gray	4073	Plate 1 x 1 Round	4211525
5		Light Bluish Gray	85861	Plate 1 x 1 Round with Open Stud	6124825, 6168647
2		Dark Bluish Gray	18674	Plate 2 x 2 Round with 1 Centre Stud	6115080

Quantity		Color	Element	Element Name	LEGO® Number
3		Light Bluish Gray	4032b	Plate 2 x 2 Round with Axlehole Type 2	4211475
1		Light Bluish Gray	60474	Plate 4 x 4 Round with Hole and Snapstud	4515351
1		Dark Bluish Gray	6587	Technic Axle 3 with Stud	4211086, 6129590, 6587199
1		Light Bluish Gray	41531	Technic Cylinder 4 x 4 x 2 with 3 Pin Holes and Center Bar	4507052
1		Light Bluish Gray	2723	Technic Disc 3 x 3 with Axlehole	
2		Light Bluish Gray	4274	Technic Pin 1/2	4211483, 4274194
1		Light Bluish Gray	4697b	Technic Pneumatic T-Piece - Type 2	4211508
1		Light Bluish Gray	32187	Technic Transmission Driving Ring Extension	4278756

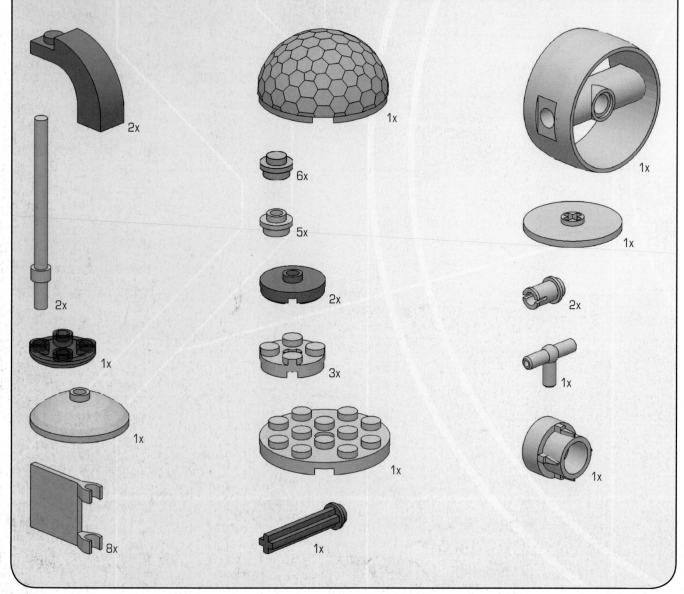

2x

1x

6x

5x

2x

2x

1x

1x

2x

3x

1x

1x

1x

8x

1x

MINI OPTIMUS PRIME

You can also easily replicate other mini-models by following the instructions for the model of this truck. Try to make a mini-Bumblebee, for example. In Joe's first book, Build Your Own City, you will find building instructions that will help you over any difficulties. Here we're going to show you how to make a mini-version of Optimus Prime, however.

In the photo you can see where the Ark crashed on Mount St. Hilary. This is the starting point for all the missions undertaken by Optimus Prime and his Autobots. In the scene we used an old base plate in dark orange, which was part of the packaging for a LEGO® set. It makes a really good mountain in our diorama.

The set was made in 1998 and has the number 6589; the base plate number is 4116414.

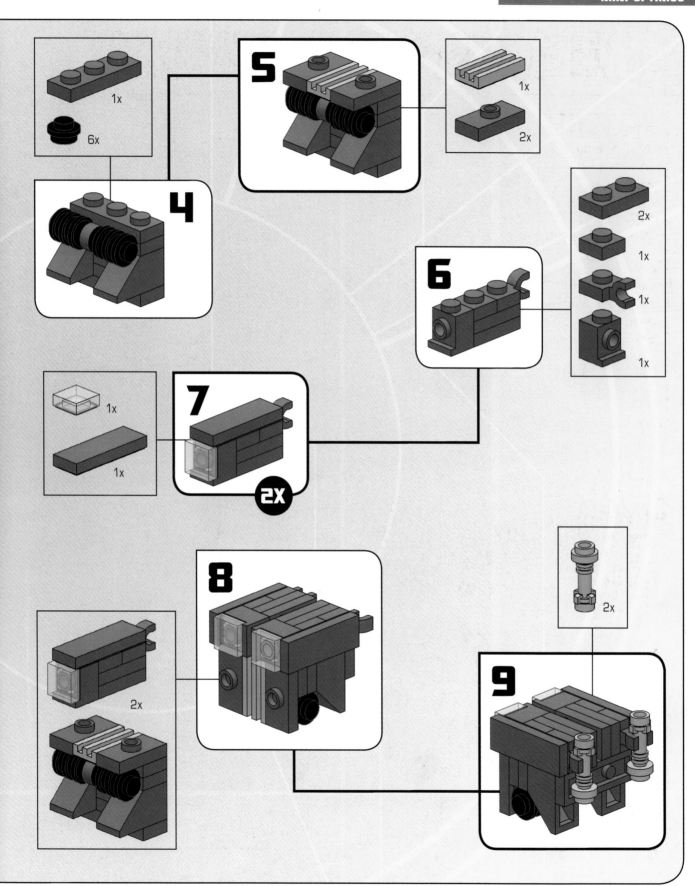

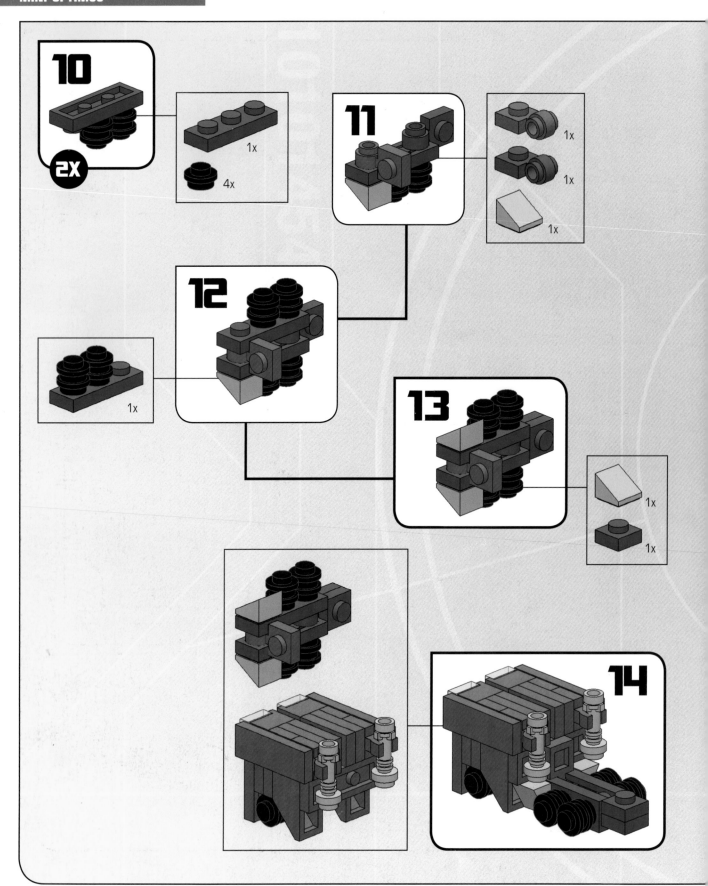

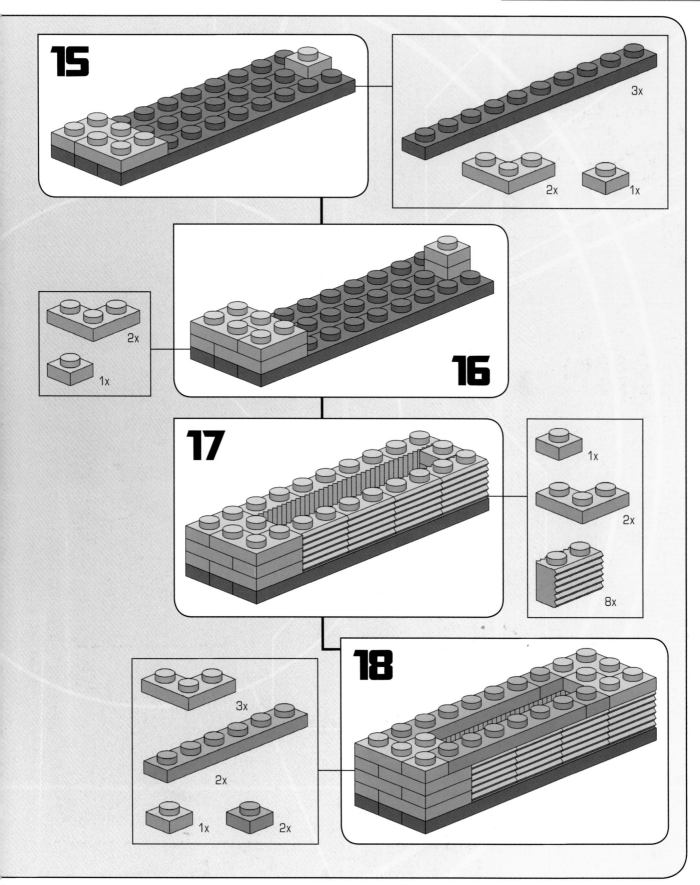

15

3x

2x

1x

2x

1x

16

17

1x

2x

8x

18

3x

2x

1x

2x

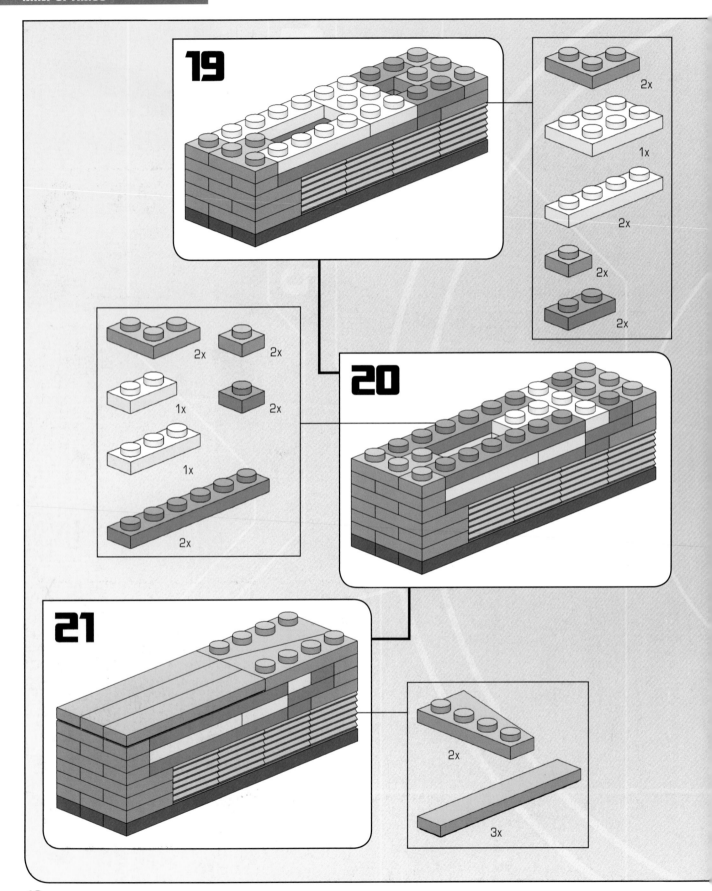

22

1x

1x

23 2X

1x

6x

2x

24

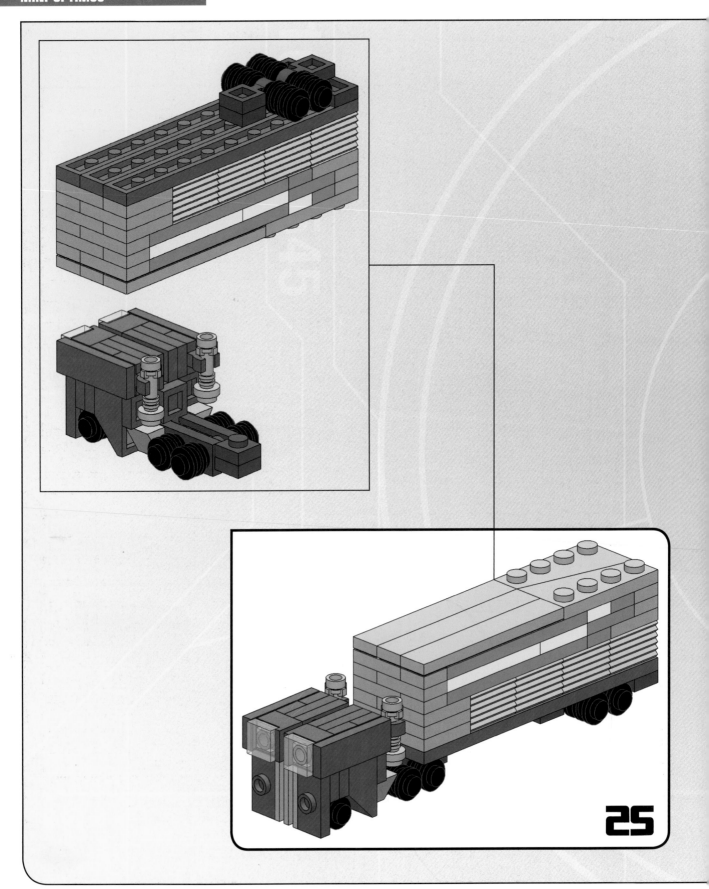

25

PARTS LIST

Quantity		Color	Element	Element Name	LEGO® Number
2		Red	4070	Brick 1 x 1 with Headlight	407021
8		Light Bluish Gray	2877	Brick 1 x 2 with Grille	4211383
2		Metallic Silver	577b	Minifig Lightsaber Hilt with Bottom Ring	
2		Blue	3024	Plate 1 x 1	302423
4		Medium Blue	3024	Plate 1 x 1	4179826
8		Metallic Silver	3024	Plate 1 x 1	4528732
8		Red	3024	Plate 1 x 1	302421
26		Black	4073	Plate 1 x 1 Round	614126
2		Red	6019	Plate 1 x 1 with Clip Horizontal (Open U-Clip)	601921
1		Red	4081a	Plate 1 x 1 with Clip Light Type 1	
3		Blue	4081b	Plate 1 x 1 with Clip Light Type 2	408123, 4632567
3		Red	4081b	Plate 1 x 1 with Clip Light Type 2	4161412, 4632572
2		Medium Blue	3023	Plate 1 x 2	4179825
4		Red	3023	Plate 1 x 2	302321
1		White	3023	Plate 1 x 2	302301
2		Red	3794	Plate 1 x 2 without Groove with 1 Centre Stud	379421
3		Blue	3623	Plate 1 x 3	362323
2		Red	3623	Plate 1 x 3	362321
1		White	3623	Plate 1 x 3	362301
2		White	3710	Plate 1 x 4	371001
4		Medium Blue	3666	Plate 1 x 6	4179829
3		Dark Bluish Gray	4477	Plate 1 x 10	4257526
13		Metallic Silver	2420	Plate 2 x 2 Corner	4528731
1		White	3021	Plate 2 x 3	302101
2		Metallic Silver	54200	Slope Brick 31 1 x 1 x 0.667	4528609, 6092109
4		Red	3040	Slope Brick 45 2 x 1	4121934
2		Trans Light Blue	3070b	Tile 1 x 1 with Groove	4175010, 6051921
1		Metallic Silver	2412b	Tile 1 x 2 Grille with Groove	4249040, 51815301, 6051422
2		Red	63864	Tile 1 x 3 with Groove	4533742
3		Metallic Silver	6636	Tile 1 x 6	4528730
2		Metallic Silver	41770	Wing 2 x 4 Left	4528772

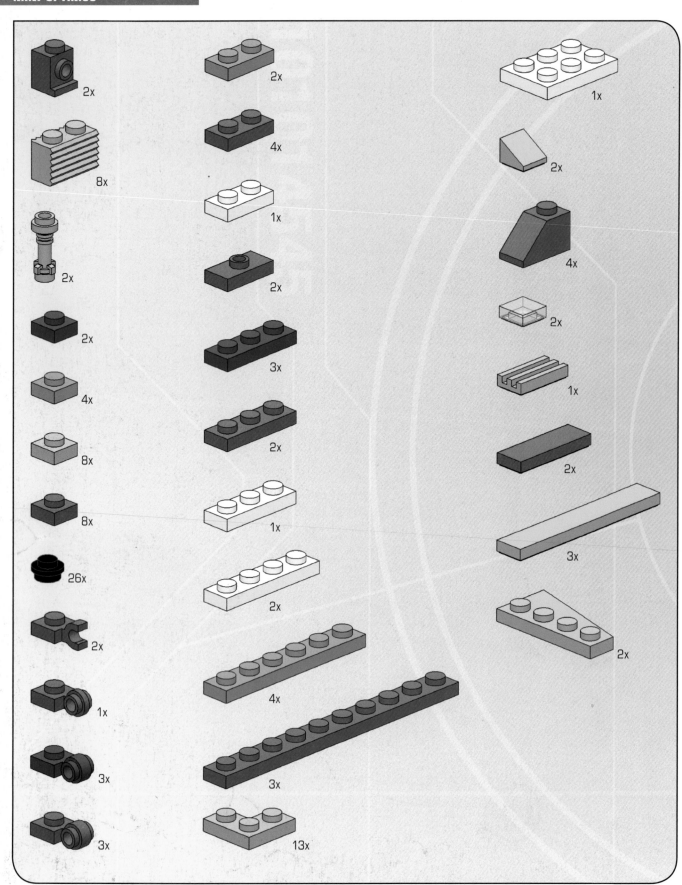

MINI-GRIMLOCK

Wheeljack is the Autobots' leading technician. He develops new ideas and weapon systems. During renovations to the Ark he finds old dinosaur bones and uses them to work out plans for turning robots into dinosaurs—Dinobots.

We've included building instructions for the little Dinobot Grimlock, whom you can see on the table.

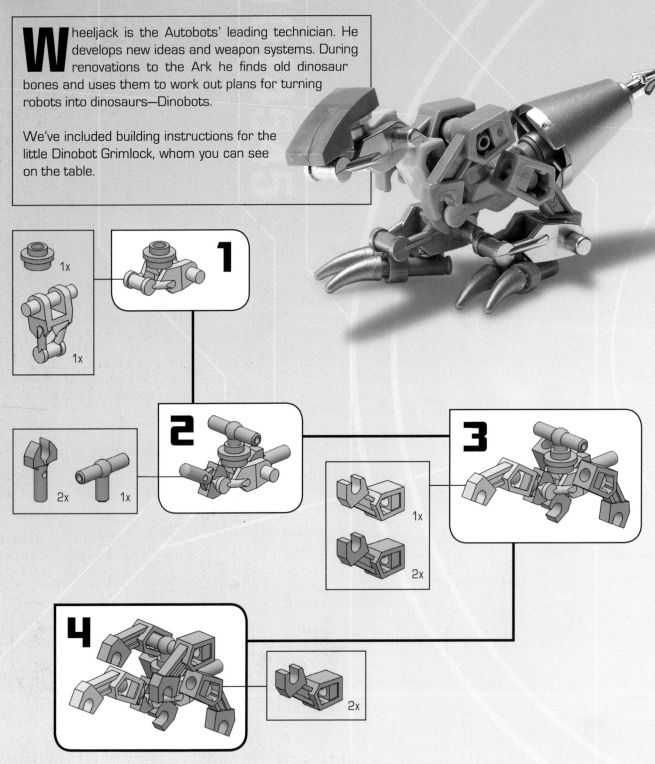

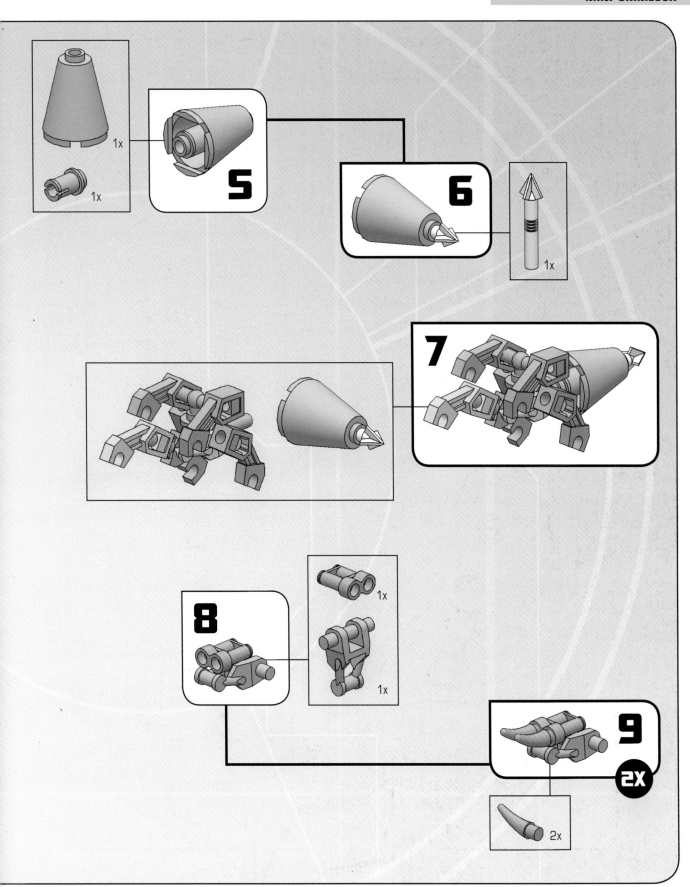

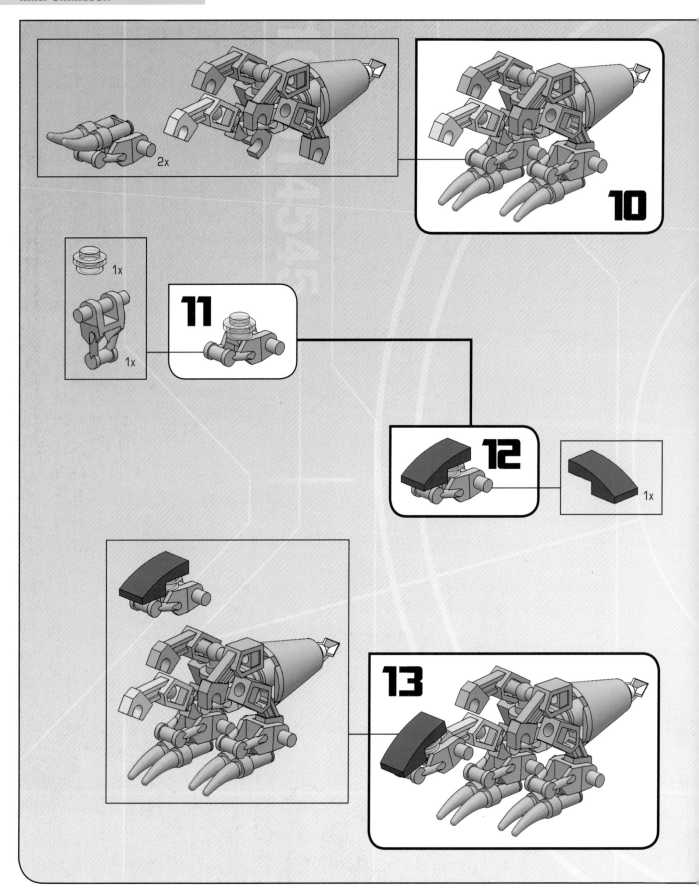

PARTS LIST

Quantity		Color	Element	Element Name	LEGO® Number
2		Pearl Light Gray	48729b	Bar 1.5L with Clip with Truncated Sides and Hole in Shaft	4529339, 4569620
1		Metallic Silver	3942c	Cone 2 x 2 x 2 with Hollow Stud Open	4528919
2		Pearl Gold	30162	Minifig Binoculars with Round Eyepiece	6034543
1		Chrome Silver	57467	Minifig Harpoon	70750
4		Pearl Gold	53451	Minifig Helmet Viking Horn	4618195
4		Pearl Light Gray	53989	Minifig Mechanical Arm with Clip and Rod Hole	4288114, 4494600
1		Yellow	53989	Minifig Mechanical Arm with Clip and Rod Hole	
3		Metallic Silver	30375	Minifig Mechanical Torso	4290382, 4540528, 4547962
1		Yellow	30375	Minifig Mechanical Torso	4224266, 4521511
1		Trans Light Blue	4073	Plate 1 x 1 Round	4163917
1		Light Bluish Gray	85861	Plate 1 x 1 Round with Open Stud	6124825, 6168647
1		Flat Silver	11477	Slope Brick Curved 2 x 1	6047418
1		Light Bluish Gray	4274	Technic Pin 1/2	4211483, 4274194
1		Light Bluish Gray	4697b	Technic Pneumatic T-Piece - Type 2	4211508

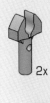
2x

1x

2x

1x

4x

4x

1x

3x

1x

1x

1x

1x

1x

1x

BUMBLEBEE

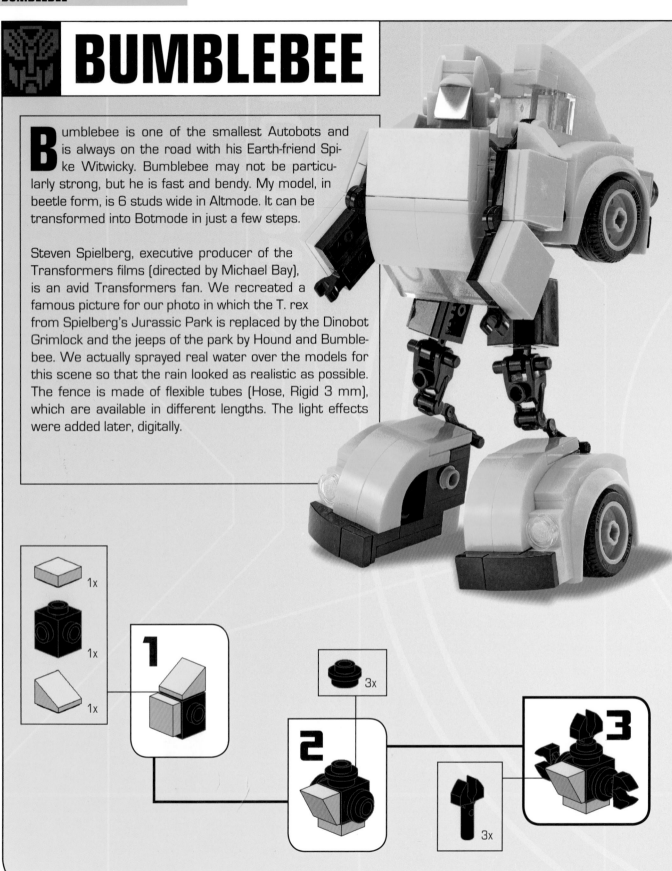

Bumblebee is one of the smallest Autobots and is always on the road with his Earth-friend Spike Witwicky. Bumblebee may not be particularly strong, but he is fast and bendy. My model, in beetle form, is 6 studs wide in Altmode. It can be transformed into Botmode in just a few steps.

Steven Spielberg, executive producer of the Transformers films (directed by Michael Bay), is an avid Transformers fan. We recreated a famous picture for our photo in which the T. rex from Spielberg's Jurassic Park is replaced by the Dinobot Grimlock and the jeeps of the park by Hound and Bumblebee. We actually sprayed real water over the models for this scene so that the rain looked as realistic as possible. The fence is made of flexible tubes (Hose, Rigid 3 mm), which are available in different lengths. The light effects were added later, digitally.

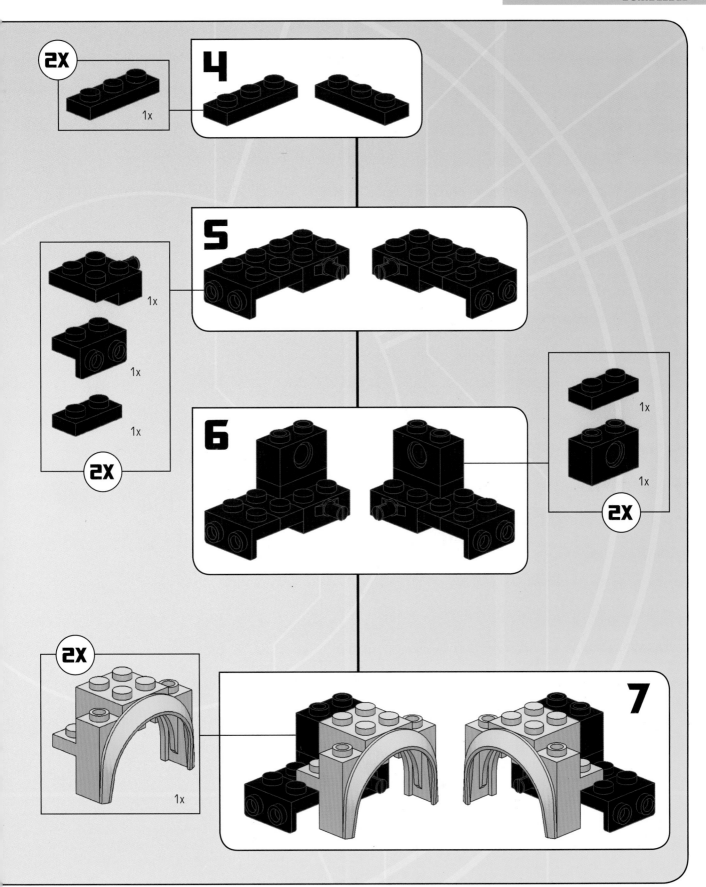

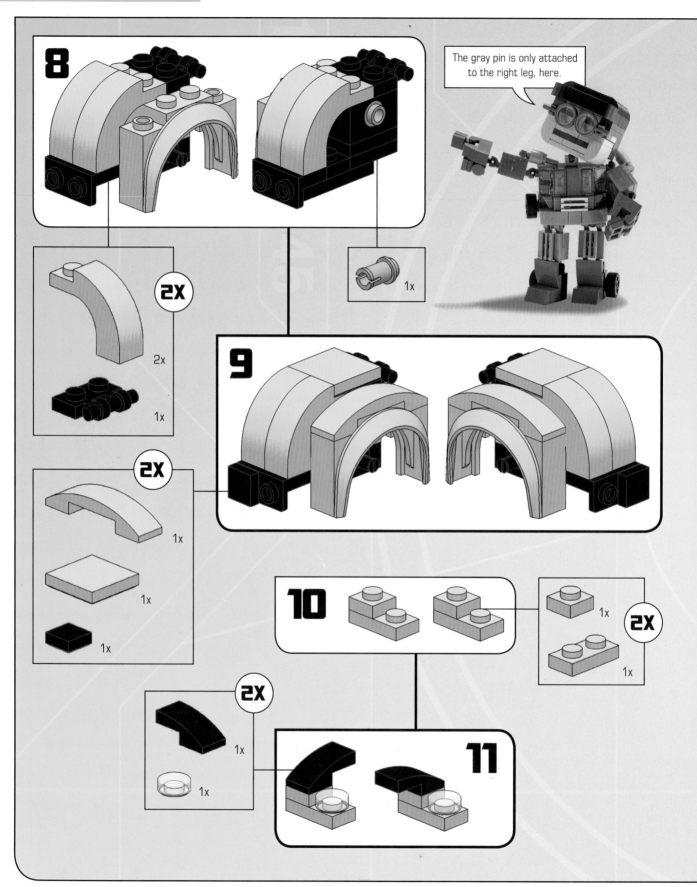

The gray pin is only attached to the right leg, here.

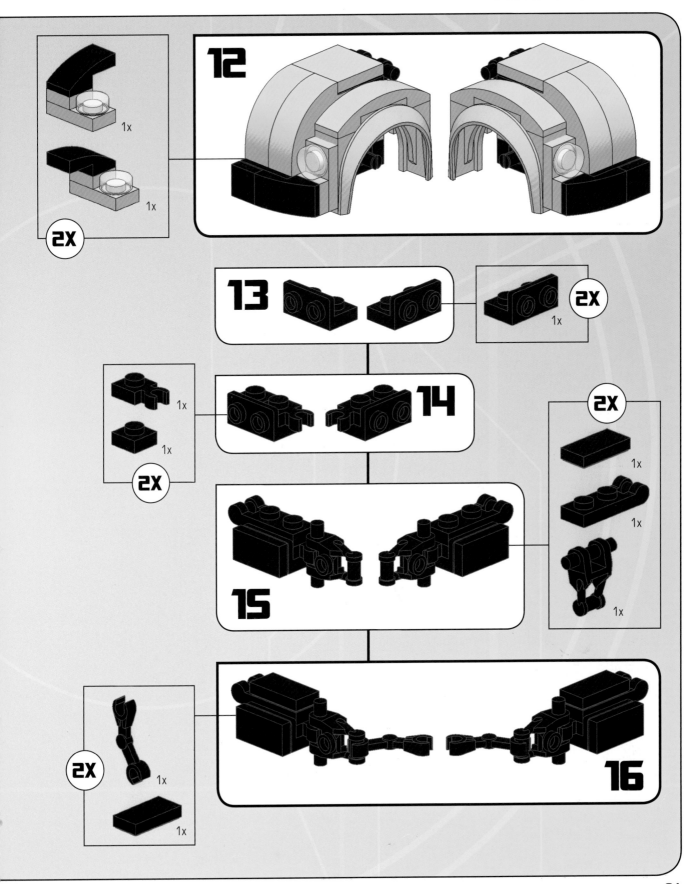

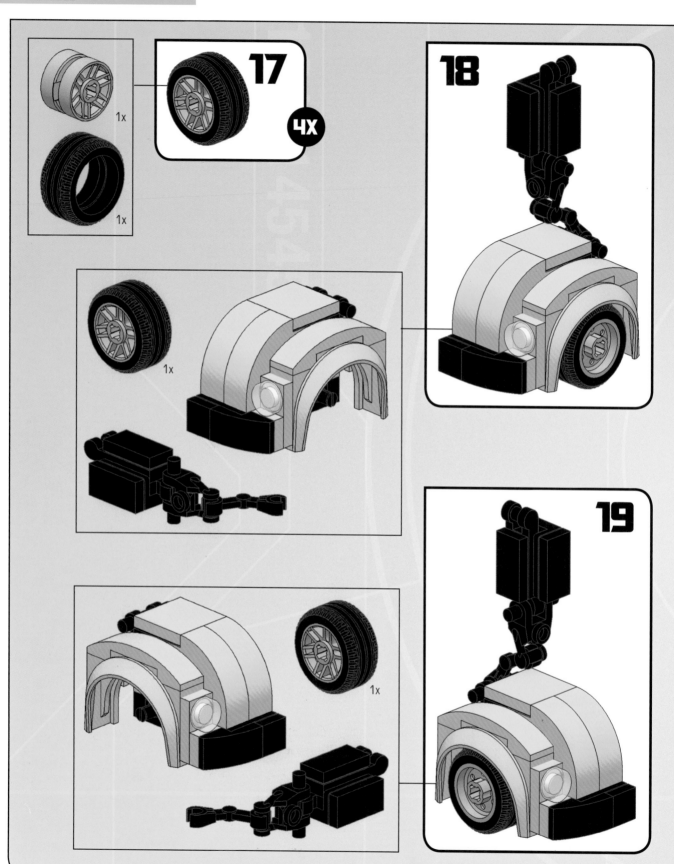

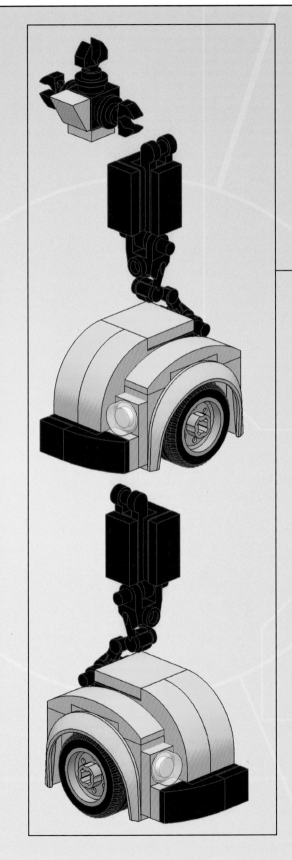

20

21

2x

22

1x

1x

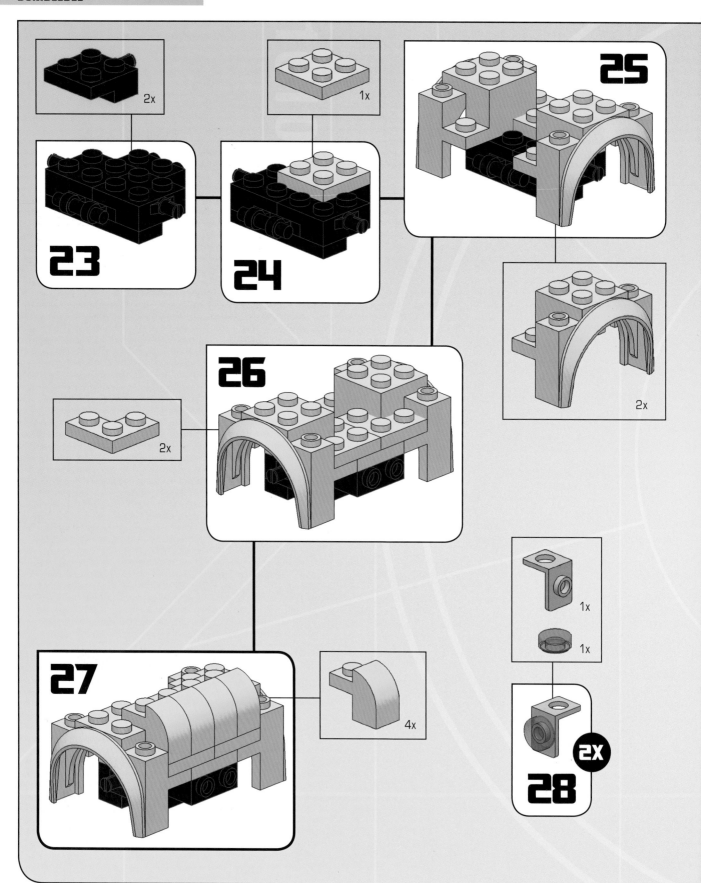

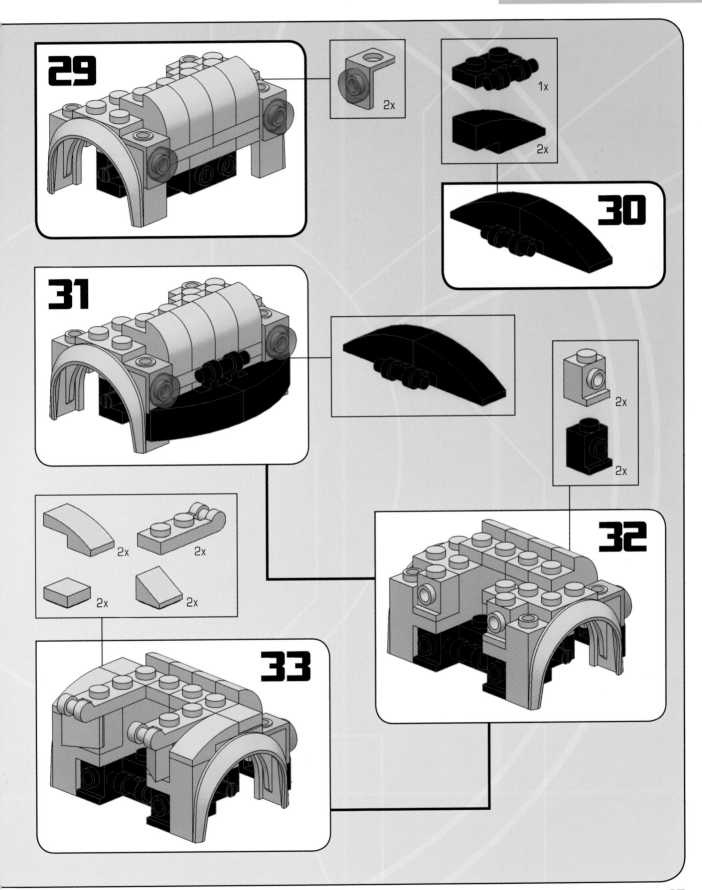

29

30

31

32

33

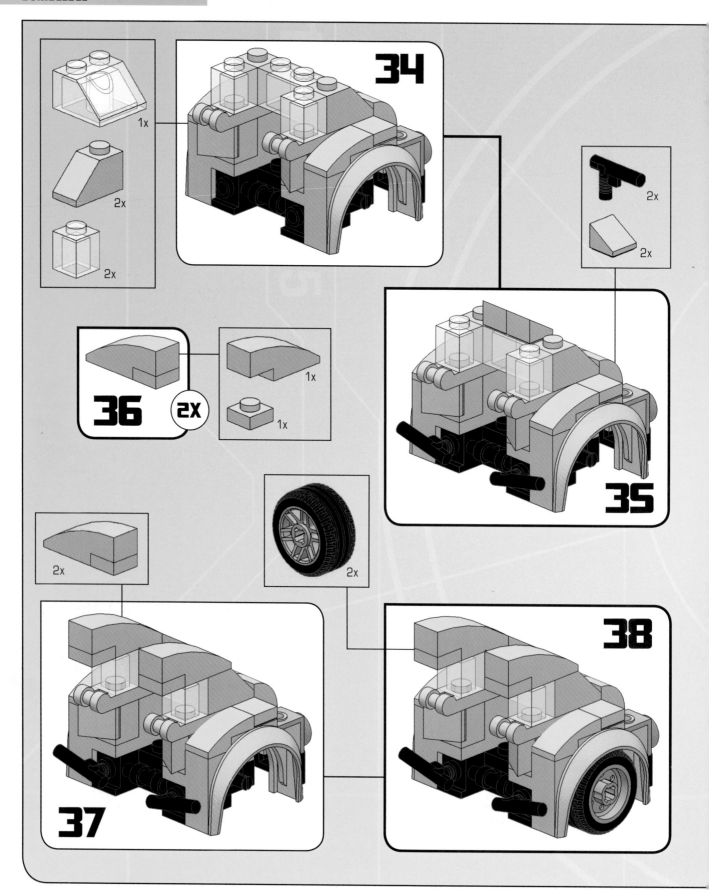

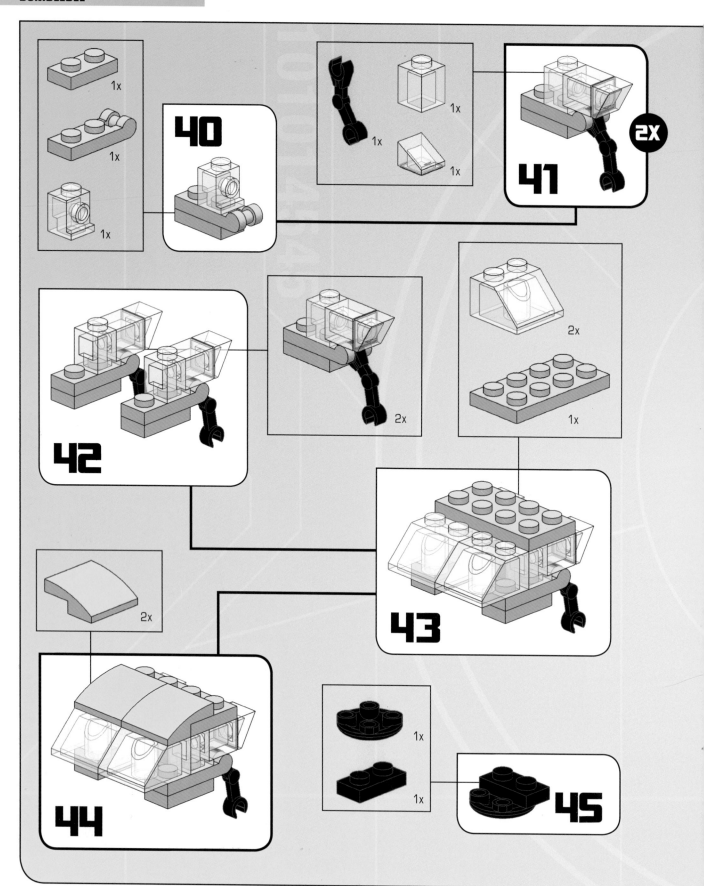

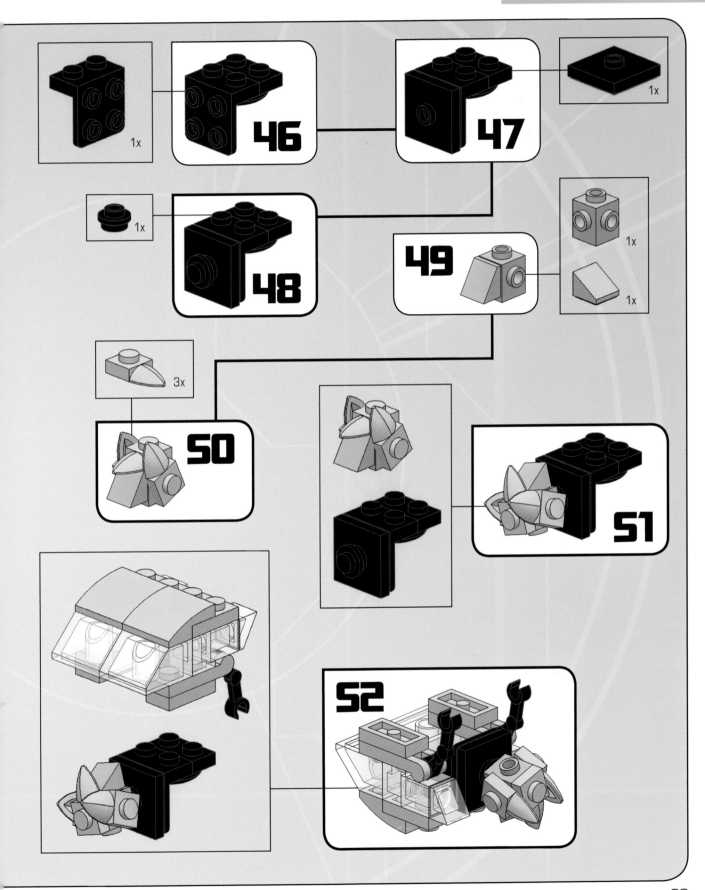

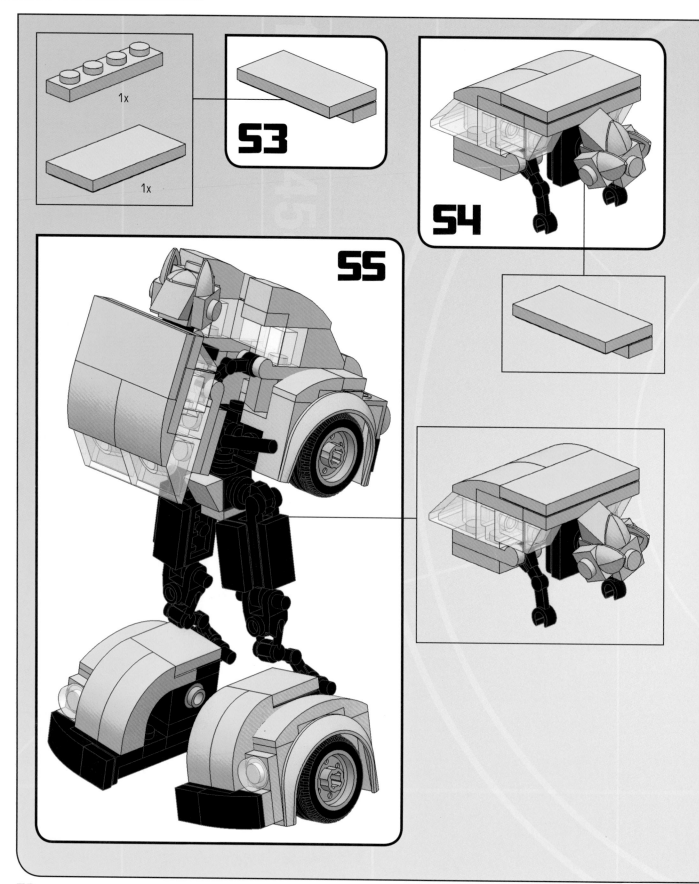

1x

1x

S3

S4

S5

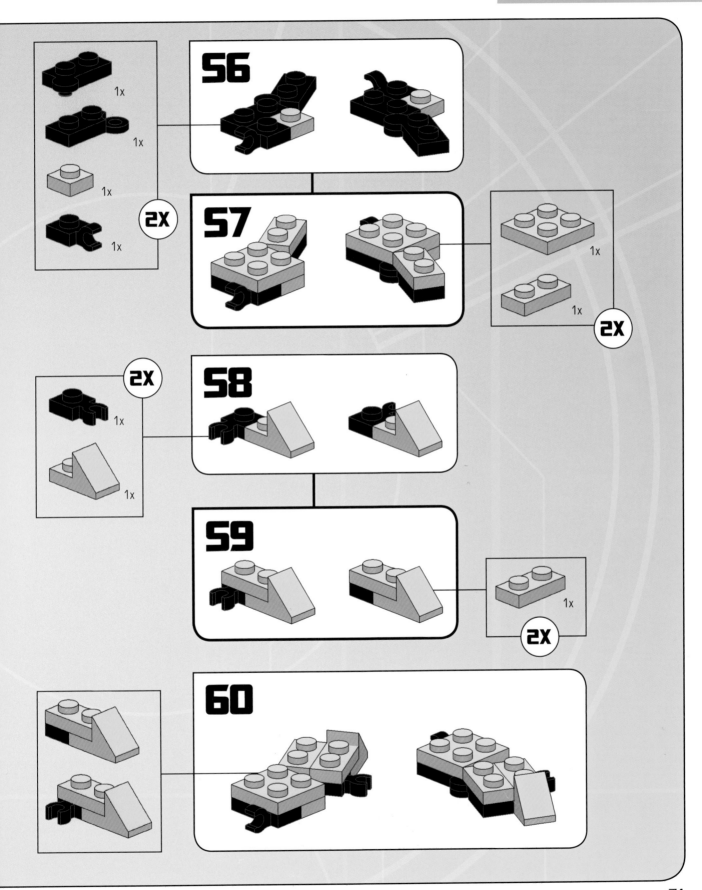

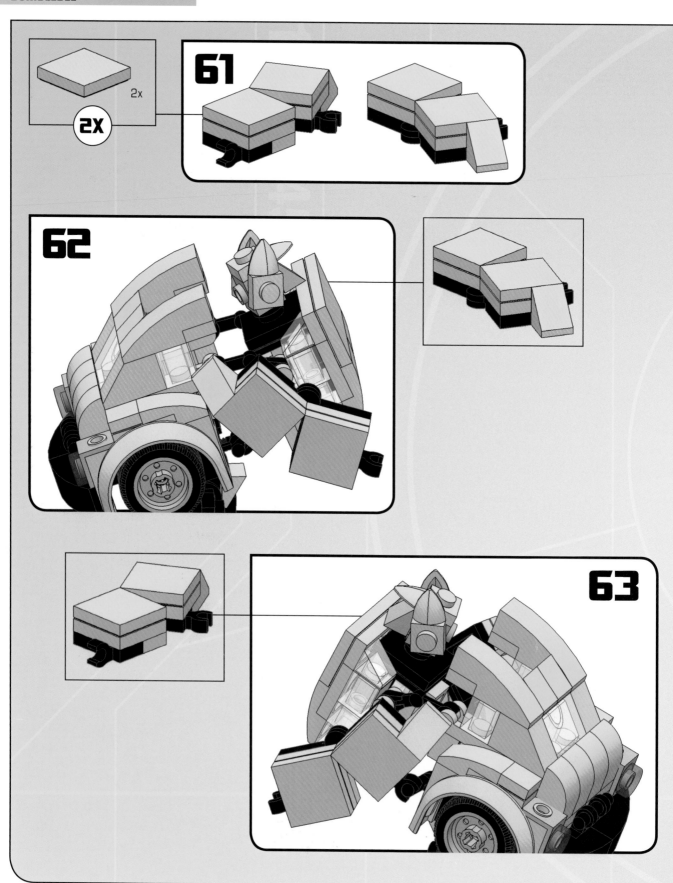

64

It's strange that Bumblebee was already known by this name on Cybertron considering that there were no bumblebees there!

Hmm, maybe the Cybertron language just doesn't translate easily and the names are all just rough equivalents. Small, yellow, nimble and quick...!

PARTS LIST

Quantity	Color		Element	Element Name	LEGO® Number
4		Bright Light Orange	6005	Arch 1 x 3 x 2 with Curved Top	6035590, 6175161
3		Black	48729b	Bar 1.5L with Clip with Truncated Sides and Hole in Shaft	4289538
2		Light Bluish Gray	42446	Bracket 1 x 1 - 1 x 1	4211760
2		Black	99781	Bracket 1 x 2 - 1 x 2 Down	6016172
2		Black	99780	Bracket 1 x 2 - 1 x 2 Up	6020193
1		Black	44728	Bracket 1 x 2 - 2 x 2	4184645, 4277932, 6048855, 6117973
4		Trans Clear	3005	Brick 1 x 1	4238226, 4645394
2		Black	4070	Brick 1 x 1 with Headlight	407026
2		Bright Light Orange	4070	Brick 1 x 1 with Headlight	6020098, 6186006
2		Trans Clear	4070	Brick 1 x 1 with Headlight	4215618
1		Black	4733	Brick 1 x 1 with Studs on Four Sides	473326
1		Light Bluish Gray	4733	Brick 1 x 1 with Studs on Four Sides	4211511
4		Bright Light Orange	6091	Brick 2 x 1 x 1 & 1/3 with Curved Top	6023185
4		Bright Light Orange	18974	Car Mudguard 4 x 2.5 x 2.333	6103455
1		Black	2654	Dish 2 x 2	265426, 4278359, 4617551
2		Black	2429	Hinge Plate 1 x 4 Swivel Base	6102782
2		Black	2430	Hinge Plate 1 x 4 Swivel Top	6102782
2		Black	60849	Minifig Hose Nozzle with Side String Hole Simplified	4537551
4		Black	30377	Minifig Mechanical Arm	4223247
2		Black	30375	Minifig Mechanical Torso	4143663, 4540274
2		Black	3024	Plate 1 x 1	302426
6		Bright Light Orange	3024	Plate 1 x 1	6073040
1		Black	4073	Plate 1 x 1 Round	614126
3		Black	85861	Plate 1 x 1 Round with Open Stud	6100627, 6168646
2		Black	61252	Plate 1 x 1 with Clip Horizontal (Thick C-Clip)	4517925
4		Black	60897	Plate 1 x 1 with Clip Vertical (Thick C-Clip)	4550017
3		Bright Light Orange	49668	Plate 1 x 1 with Tooth In-line	4282860
5		Black	3023	Plate 1 x 2	302326
8		Bright Light Orange	3023	Plate 1 x 2	6028736
4		Black	2540	Plate 1 x 2 with Handle	254026, 4140588
2		Black	60478	Plate 1 x 2 with Handle on End	4515368
4		Bright Light Orange	60478	Plate 1 x 2 with Handle on End	6097507
2		Black	3623	Plate 1 x 3	362326

Quantity	Color		Element	Element Name	LEGO® Number
1		Bright Light Orange	3710	Plate 1 x 4	6020073
3		Bright Light Orange	3022	Plate 2 x 2	4243776, 6003033
2		Black	2420	Plate 2 x 2 Corner	242026
2		Bright Light Orange	2420	Plate 2 x 2 Corner	6099714
1		Black	87580	Plate 2 x 2 with Groove with 1 Center Stud	4565323
4		Black	4488	Plate 2 x 2 with Wheel Holder	448826, 6092658
1		Black	99206	Plate 2 x 2 x 0.667 with Two Studs On Side and Two Raised	6052126
1		Bright Light Orange	3020	Plate 2 x 4	6097511
5		Bright Light Orange	54200	Slope Brick 31 1 x 1 x 0.667	6023173
1		Metallic Silver	54200	Slope Brick 31 1 x 1 x 0.667	4528609, 6092109
2		Trans Clear	54200	Slope Brick 31 1 x 1 x 0.667	4244362
2		Bright Light Orange	3040	Slope Brick 45 2 x 1	6023157
3		Trans Clear	3039	Slope Brick 45 2 x 2	622740
2		Black	11477	Slope Brick Curved 2 x 1	6047276
2		Bright Light Orange	11477	Slope Brick Curved 2 x 1	6099728
2		Bright Light Orange	15068	Slope Brick Curved 2 x 2 x 0.667	6099730
2		Black	50950	Slope Brick Curved 3 x 1	4251161
2		Bright Light Orange	50950	Slope Brick Curved 3 x 1	6022064
2		Bright Light Orange	93273	Slope Brick Curved 4 x 1 Double	6133826
2		Bright Light Orange	15672	Slope Plate 45 2 x 1	6020106
2		Black	3700	Technic Brick 1 x 2 with Hole	370026
1		Light Bluish Gray	4274	Technic Pin 1/2	4211483, 4274194
2		Trans Clear	98138	Tile 1 x 1 Round with Groove	4650498
2		Trans Red	98138	Tile 1 x 1 Round with Groove	4646864
2		Black	3070b	Tile 1 x 1 with Groove	307026
3		Bright Light Orange	3070b	Tile 1 x 1 with Groove	6065504
4		Black	3069b	Tile 1 x 2 with Groove	306926
6		Bright Light Orange	3068b	Tile 2 x 2 with Groove	4525871, 6020147
1		Bright Light Orange	87079	Tile 2 x 4 with Groove	4621543
4		Black	11209	Tyre 10/ 32 x 14	6029208
4		Light Bluish Gray	11208	Wheel Rim 10 x 14 with Fake Bolts and 6 Spokes	6029209

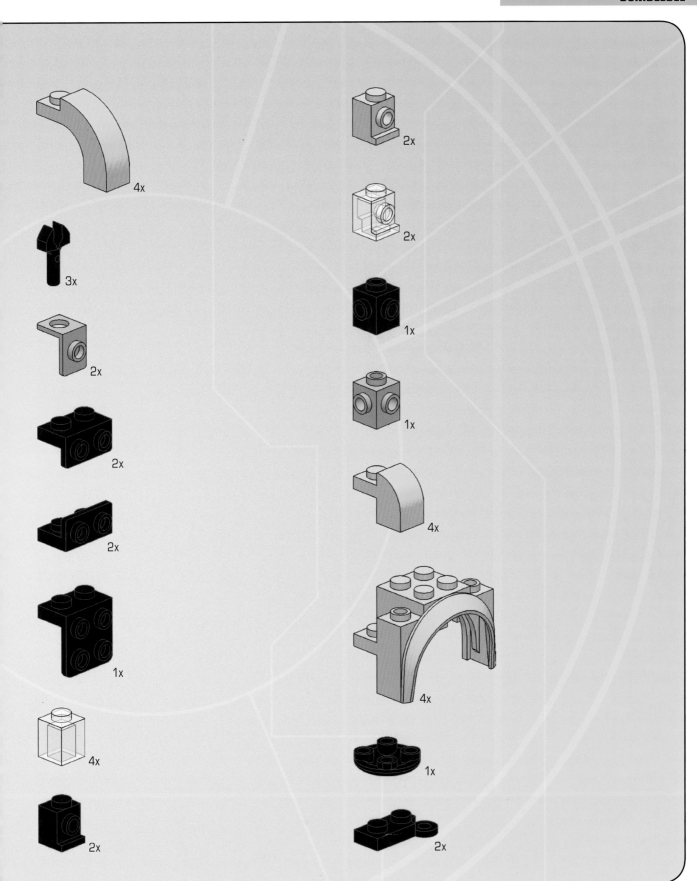

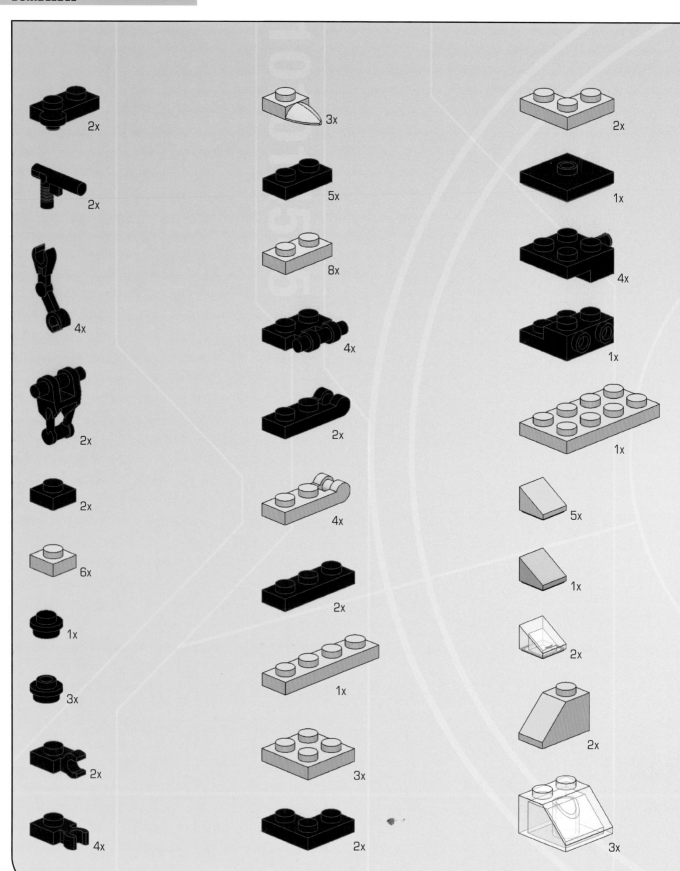

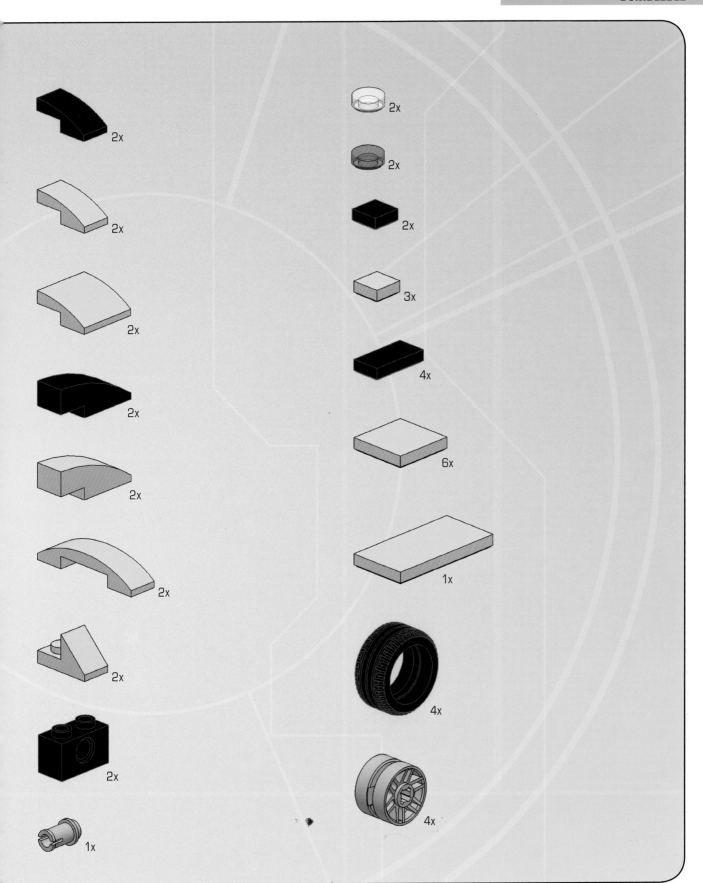

2x

2x

2x

2x

2x

2x

2x

2x

1x

2x

2x

2x

3x

4x

6x

1x

4x

4x

Addicted to energon, the Insecticons are always hungry—nothing can stop them once they discover a source of those cubes. Even Megatron, leader of the Decepticons, hadn't reckoned on their insatiable greed. Shrapnel, Kickback, and Bombshell are a well-coordinated bunch when it comes to eating through electronic circuits.

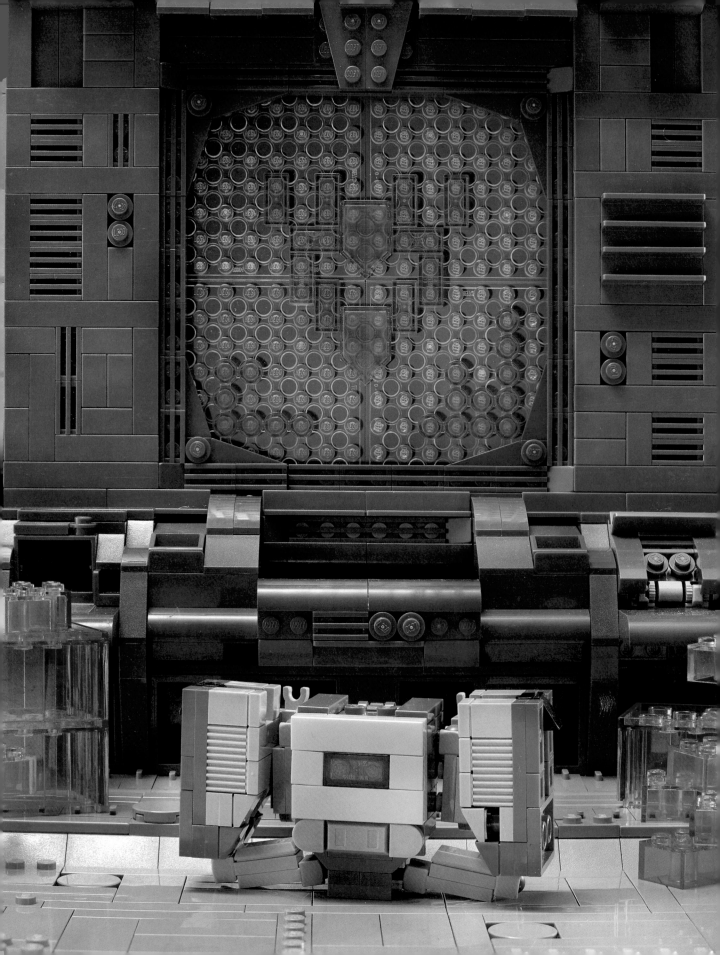

SOUNDWAVE

Soundwave is the Decepticons' communications officer. He can transform himself into a Walkman and has a talent for being a spy. In the picture you can see him at the Decepticons' headquarters with the energon cubes he's collected. We've included a small version of him for you to make.

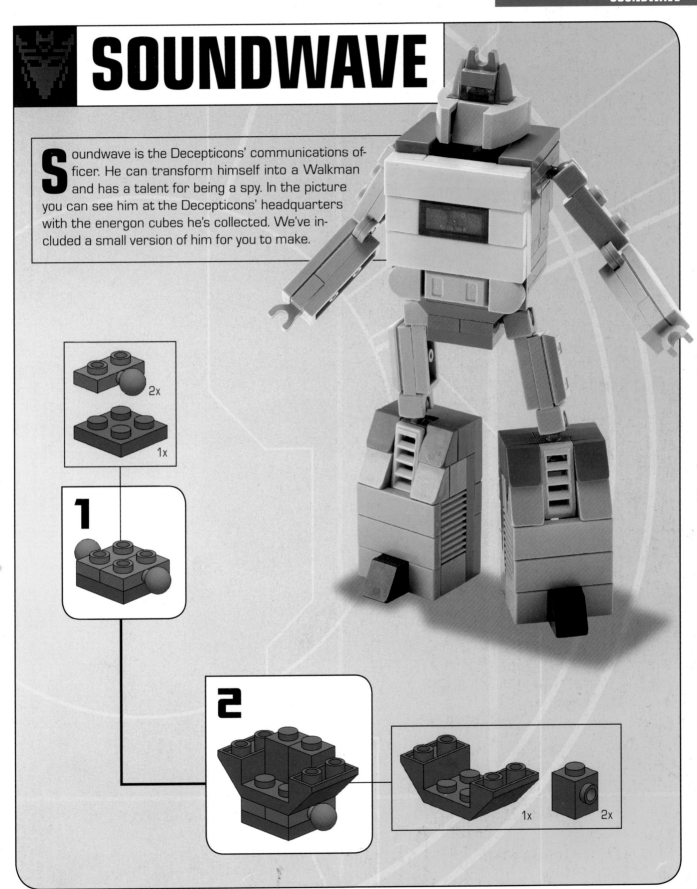

2x

1x

1

2

1x

2x

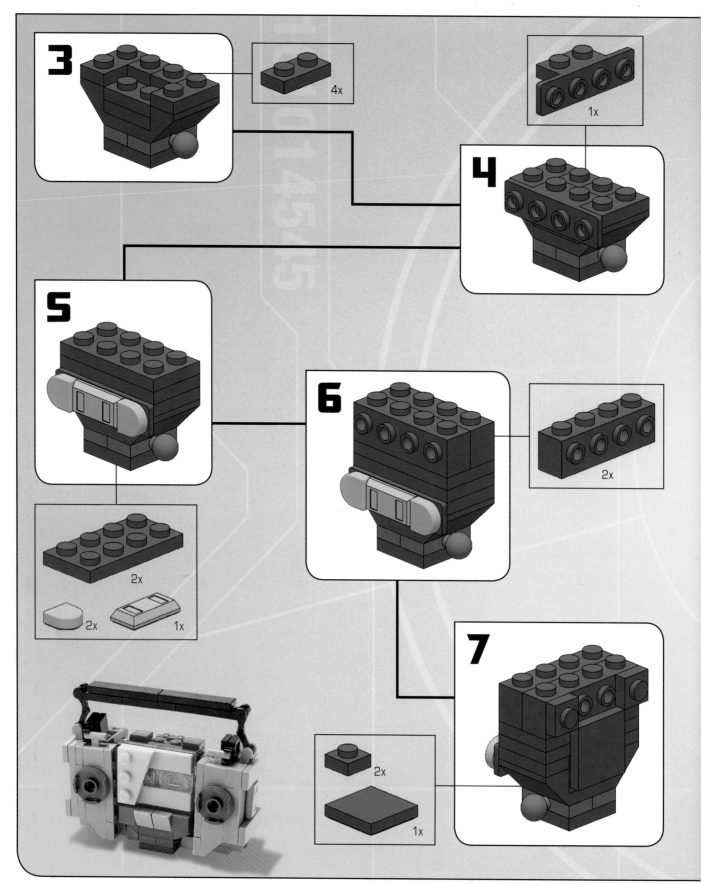

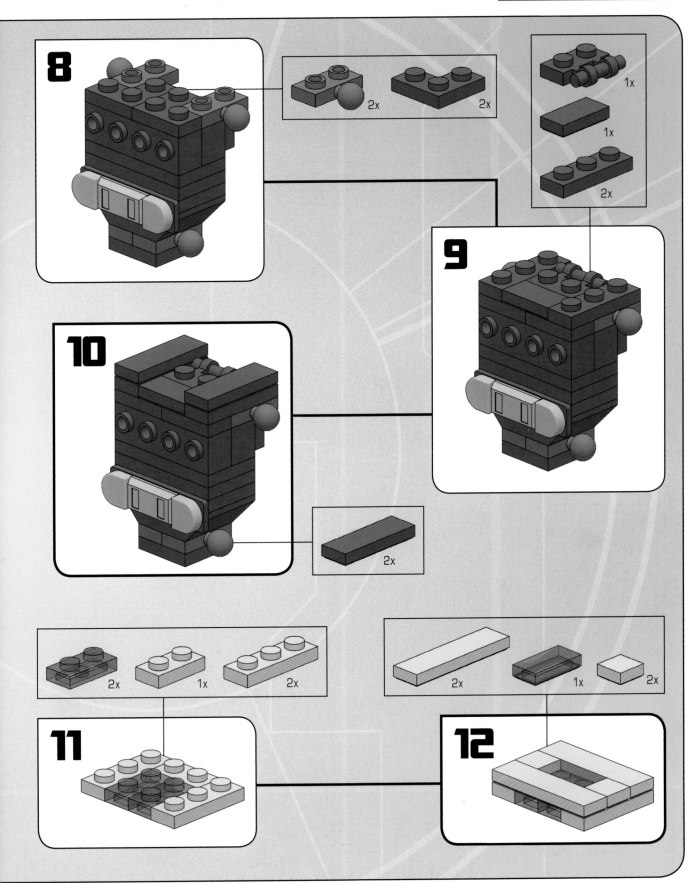

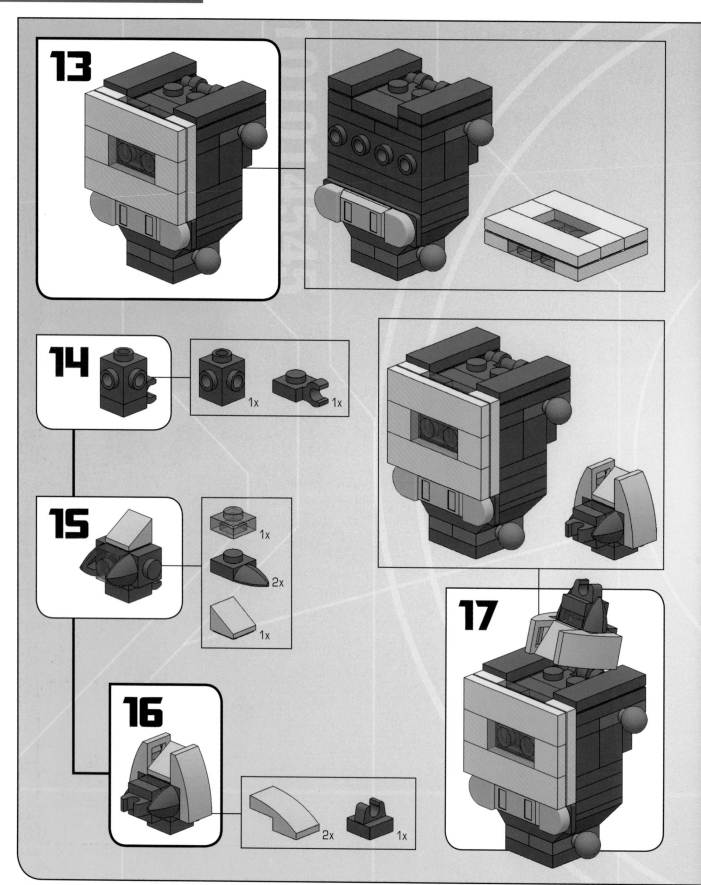

13

14

1x   1x

15

1x

2x

1x

16

17

2x   1x

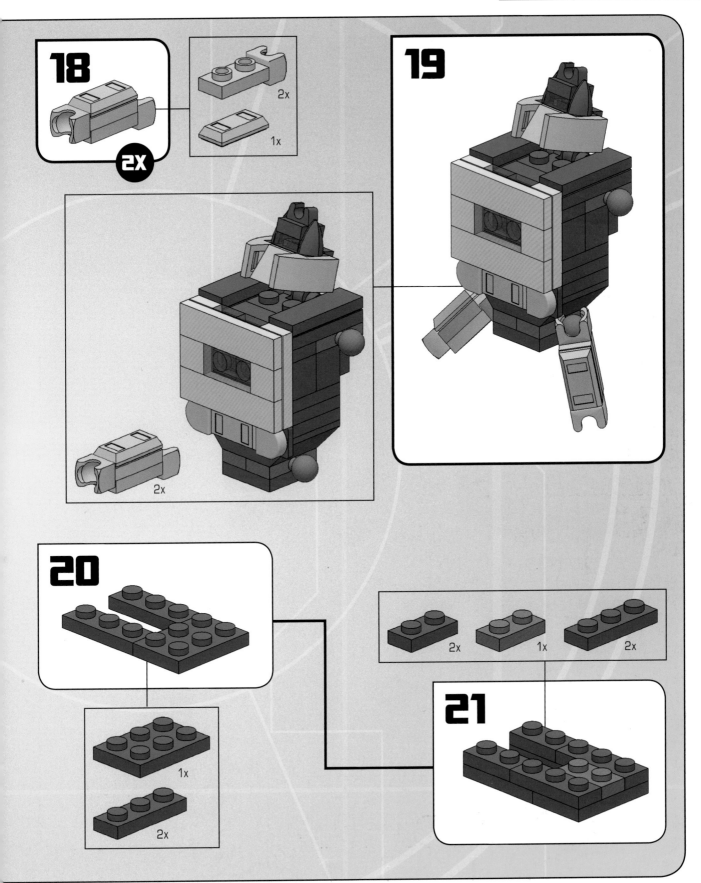

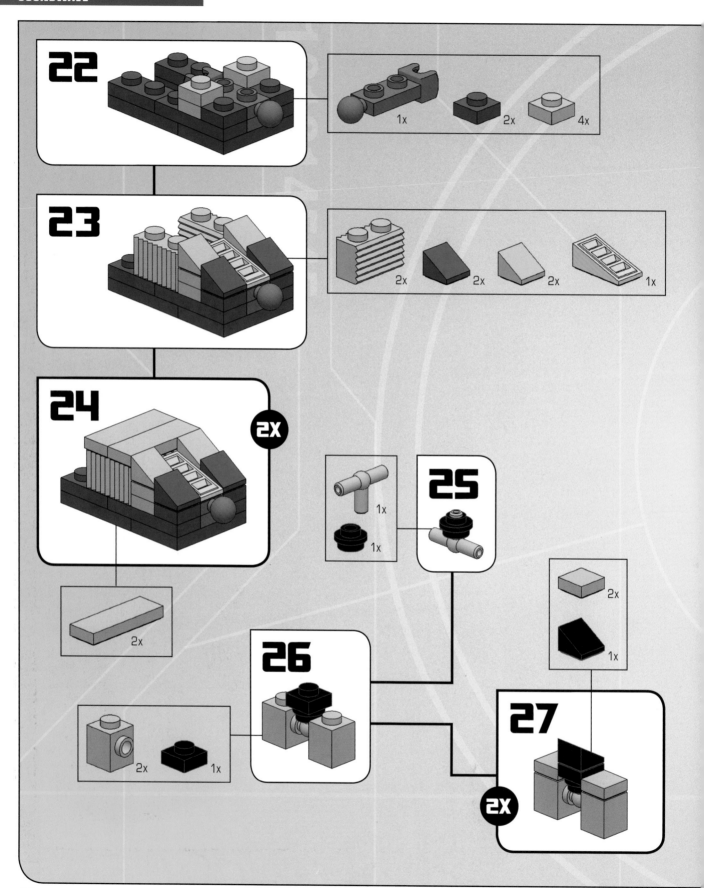

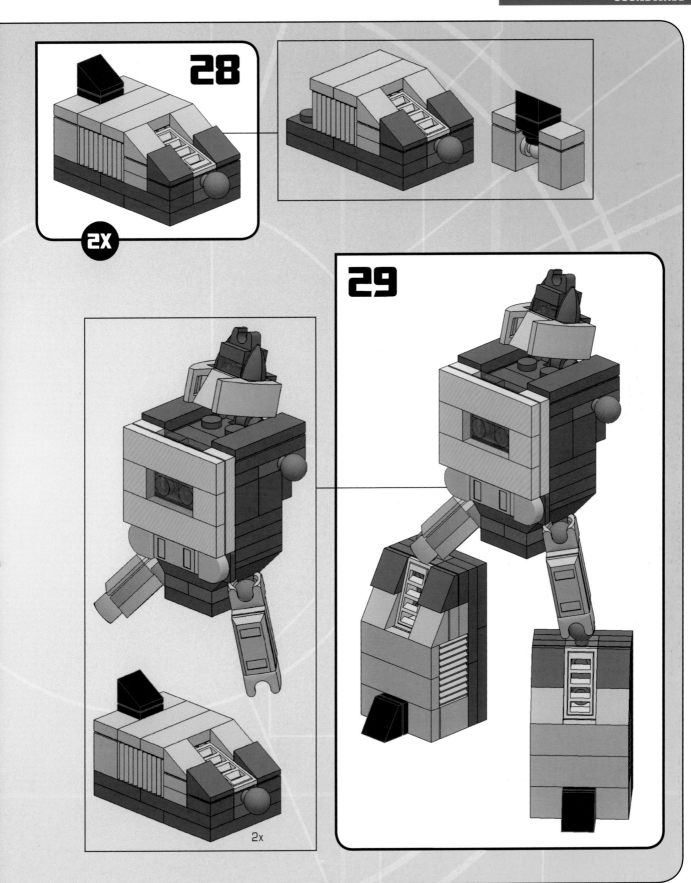

28

2X

29

2x

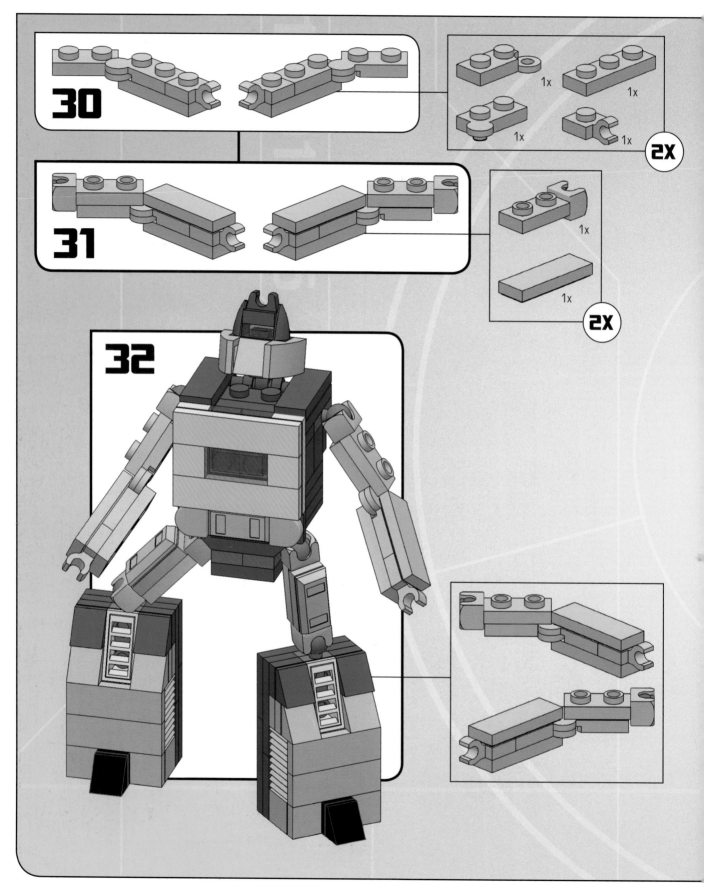

30

1x
1x
1x
1x

2X

31

1x
1x

2X

32

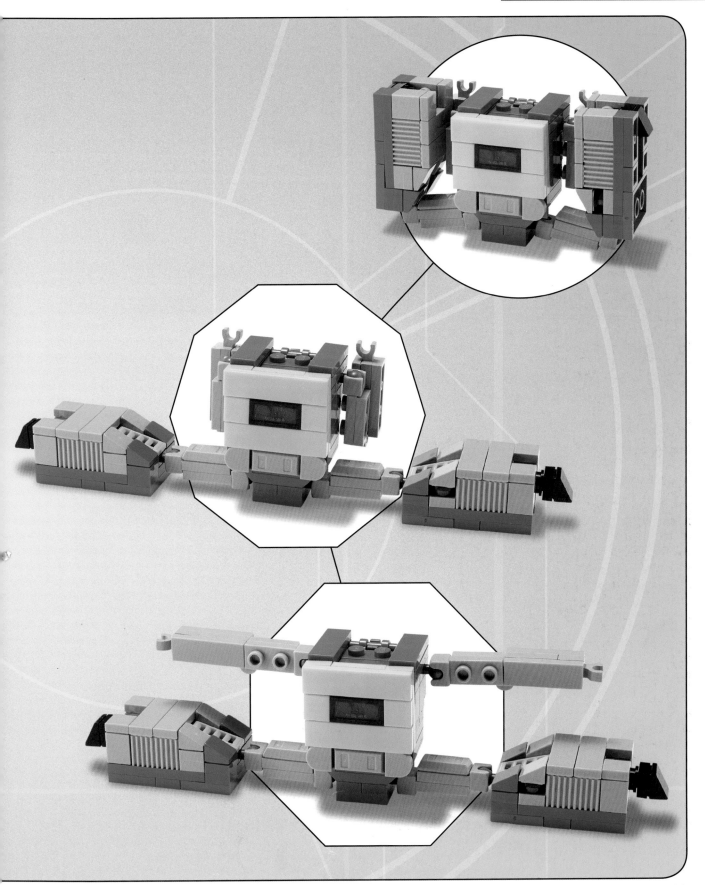

PARTS LIST

Quantity	Color	Element	Element Name	LEGO® Number
1	Blue	2436b	Bracket 1 x 2 - 1 x 4 with Rounded Corners	4282744, 6119159
2	Blue	87087	Brick 1 x 1 with Stud on 1 Side	4583862
4	Light Bluish Gray	87087	Brick 1 x 1 with Stud on 1 Side	4558953
1	Blue	4733	Brick 1 x 1 with Studs on Four Sides	4296151
4	Light Bluish Gray	2877	Brick 1 x 2 with Grille	4211383
2	Blue	30414	Brick 1 x 4 with Studs on Side	4212411
3	Light Bluish Gray	99563	Gold Ingot	6134378
2	Light Bluish Gray	2429	Hinge Plate 1 x 4 Swivel Base	4219256
2	Light Bluish Gray	2430	Hinge Plate 1 x 4 Swivel Top	
2	Black	3024	Plate 1 x 1	302426
6	Blue	3024	Plate 1 x 1	302423
8	Light Bluish Gray	3024	Plate 1 x 1	4211399
1	Trans Red	3024	Plate 1 x 1	3000841
2	Black	85861	Plate 1 x 1 Round with Open Stud	6100627, 6168646
1	Blue	61252	Plate 1 x 1 with Clip Horizontal (Thick C-Clip)	4520946
2	Light Bluish Gray	61252	Plate 1 x 1 with Clip Horizontal (Thick C-Clip)	4541978
2	Blue	49668	Plate 1 x 1 with Tooth In-line	4247040, 6123860
8	Blue	3023	Plate 1 x 2	302323
2	Dark Bluish Gray	3023	Plate 1 x 2	4211063
2	Trans Black	3023	Plate 1 x 2	6001197
1	Yellow	3023	Plate 1 x 2	302324
4	Dark Bluish Gray	14417	Plate 1 x 2 with Ball Joint-8	6039479
1	Blue	2540	Plate 1 x 2 with Handle	254023, 4140586
6	Light Bluish Gray	14418	Plate 1 x 2 with Socket Joint-8 with Friction	6043639
2	Dark Bluish Gray	14419	Plate 1 x 2 with Socket Joint-8 with Friction and Ball Joint-8	6039482
10	Blue	3623	Plate 1 x 3	362323
2	Light Bluish Gray	3623	Plate 1 x 3	3623194, 4211429
2	Yellow	3623	Plate 1 x 3	362324
1	Blue	3022	Plate 2 x 2	302223, 4613973
2	Blue	2420	Plate 2 x 2 Corner	242023
2	Blue	3021	Plate 2 x 3	302123
2	Blue	3020	Plate 2 x 4	302023
2	Yellow	61409	Slope Brick 18 2 x 1 x 2/3 Grille	4521167, 4540384
2	Black	54200	Slope Brick 31 1 x 1 x 0.667	4287159, 4504382

Quantity	Color	Element	Element Name	LEGO® Number
4	Blue	54200	Slope Brick 31 1 x 1 x 0.667	4296154, 4504380
5	Light Bluish Gray	54200	Slope Brick 31 1 x 1 x 0.667	4521921
1	Blue	4871	Slope Brick 45 4 x 2 Double Inverted with Open Centre	4189119, 4656767
2	Light Bluish Gray	11477	Slope Brick Curved 2 x 1	6028813
2	Light Bluish Gray	4697b	Technic Pneumatic T-Piece - Type 2	4211508
1	Blue	12825	Tile 1 x 1 with Clip with Rounded Tips	
4	Light Bluish Gray	3070b	Tile 1 x 1 with Groove	4211415
2	Yellow	3070b	Tile 1 x 1 with Groove	307024
2	Light Bluish Gray	24246	Tile 1 x 1 with Rounded End	6151688
1	Blue	3069b	Tile 1 x 2 with Groove	306923
1	Trans Black	3069b	Tile 1 x 2 with Groove	4250471, 4529685
2	Blue	63864	Tile 1 x 3 with Groove	4587840
6	Light Bluish Gray	63864	Tile 1 x 3 with Groove	4558169
2	Yellow	2431	Tile 1 x 4 with Groove	243124
1	Blue	3068b	Tile 2 x 2 with Groove	306823

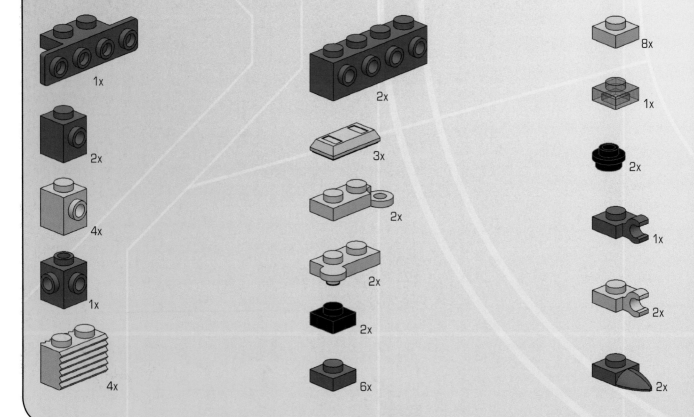

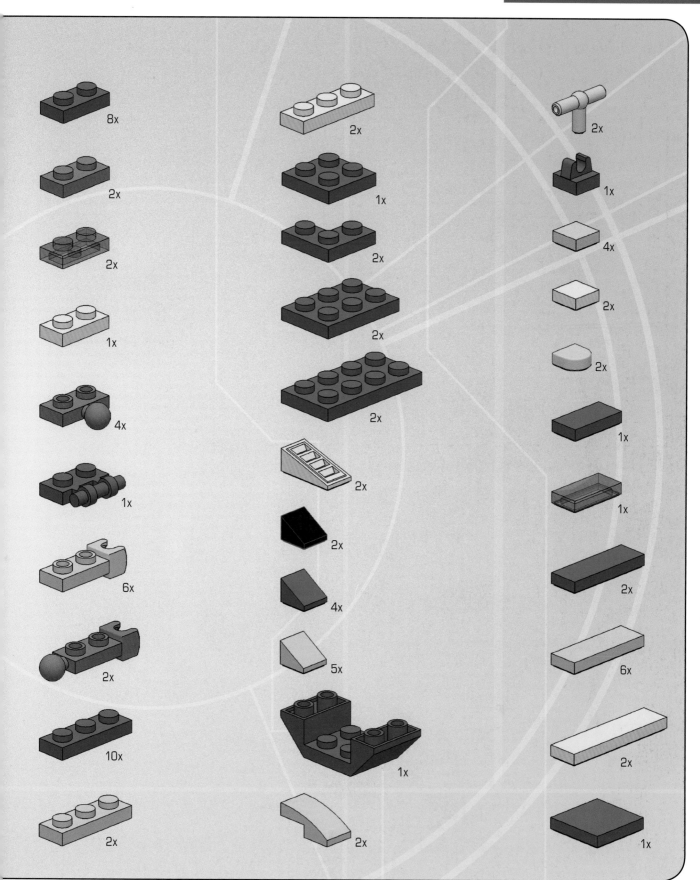

CONSTRUCTICONS

The Constructicons are the original designers, engineers, and builders of the Transformers. They are also the first group to join together to make one big robot, the Devastator, one of the most dangerous and powerful robots among the Decepticons. We'll provide you with building instructions for all six Constructicon vehicles and, of course, the additional connectors that you need. The dark-purple elements are fixed together with MIXEL Ball Joints and ensure the best robot results, which you can easily change into different poses.

BONECRUSHER

Bonecrusher, as the bulldozer component of the Devastator, turns destruction into a savage art form. Megatron just loves the fear and desolation he leaves behind—if only he could stop destroying all those things that the Decepticons desperately need...

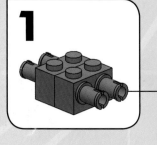

2x

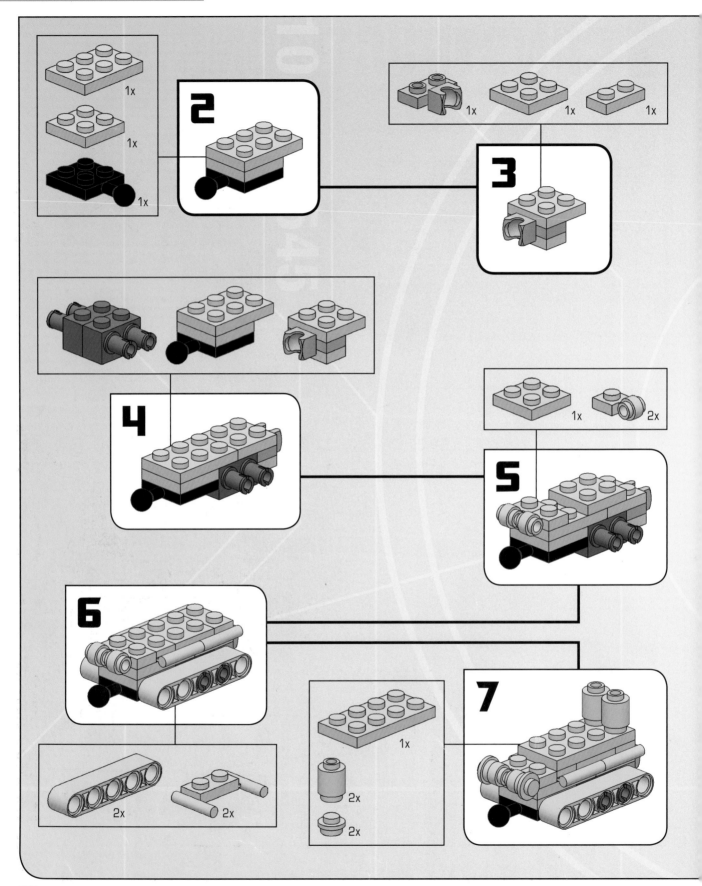

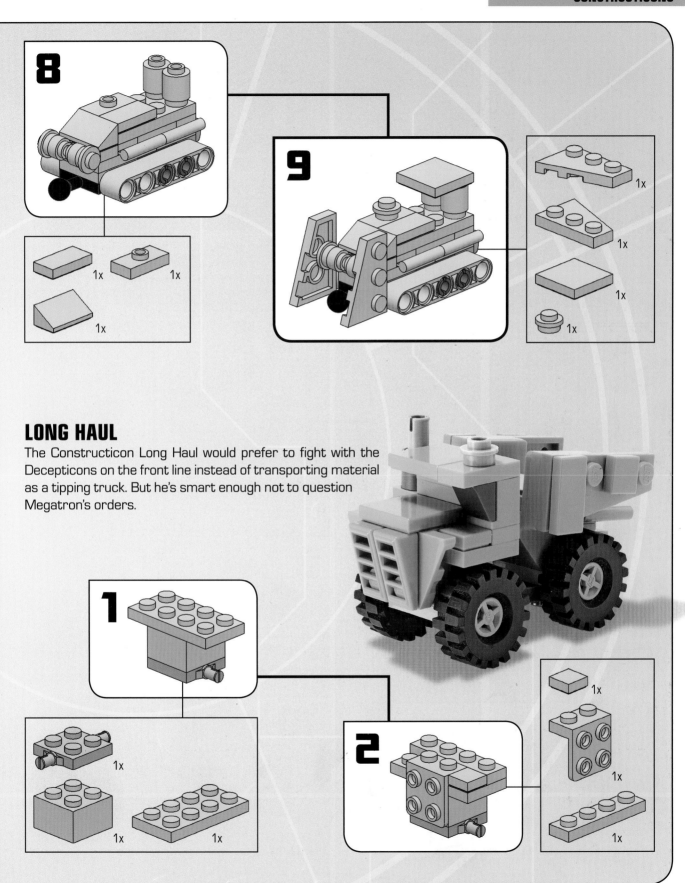

LONG HAUL

The Constructicon Long Haul would prefer to fight with the Decepticons on the front line instead of transporting material as a tipping truck. But he's smart enough not to question Megatron's orders.

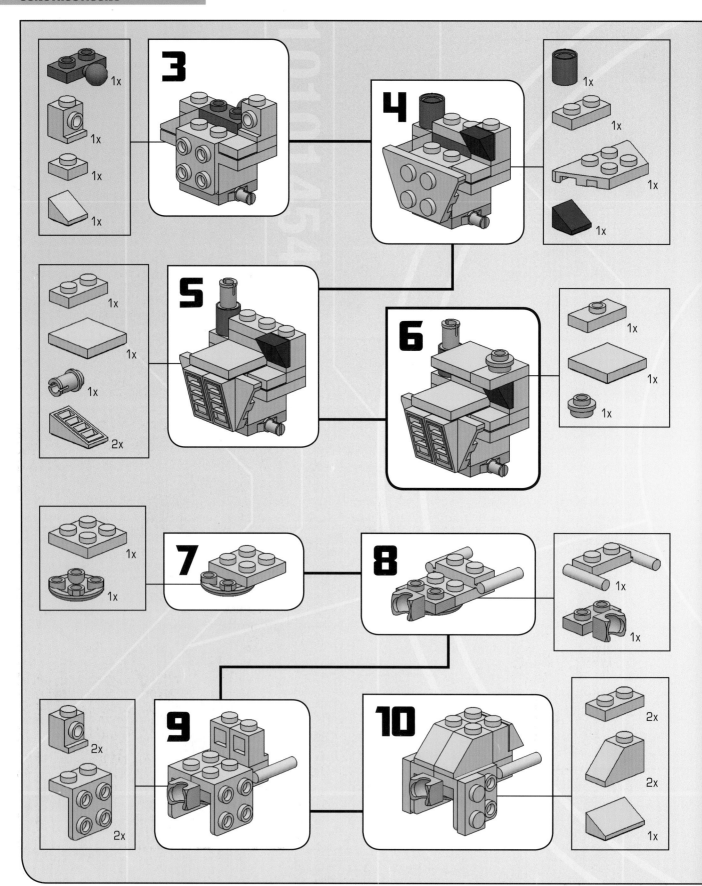

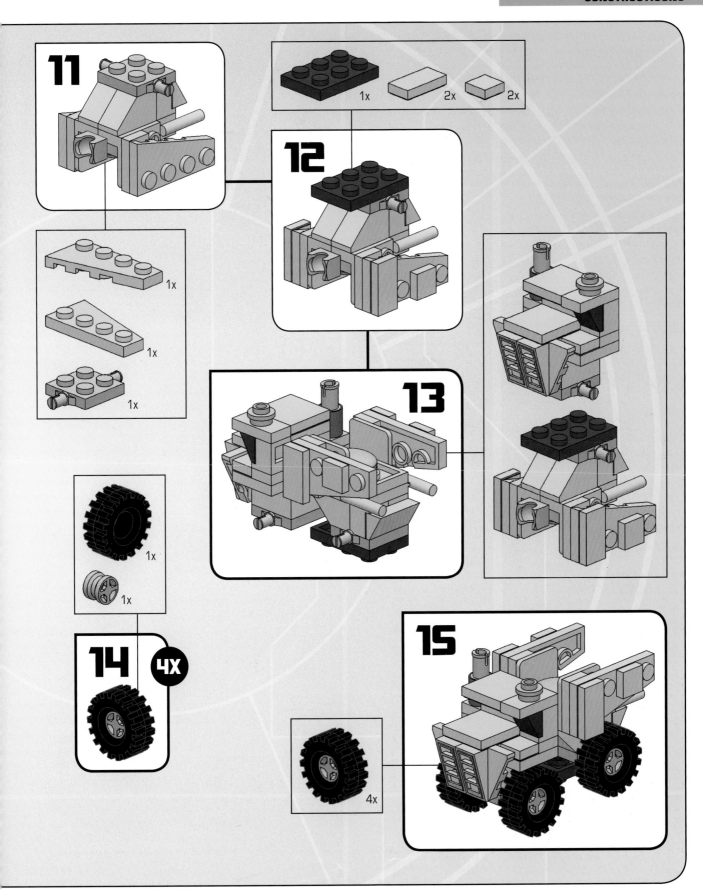

11

12

1x   2x   2x

1x

1x

1x

13

1x

1x

14 **4X**

15

4x

SCAVENGER

Scavenger has such low self-esteem that he would do almost anything to get recognition from his team. But it's precisely for this reason that they consider him to be a worthless loser.

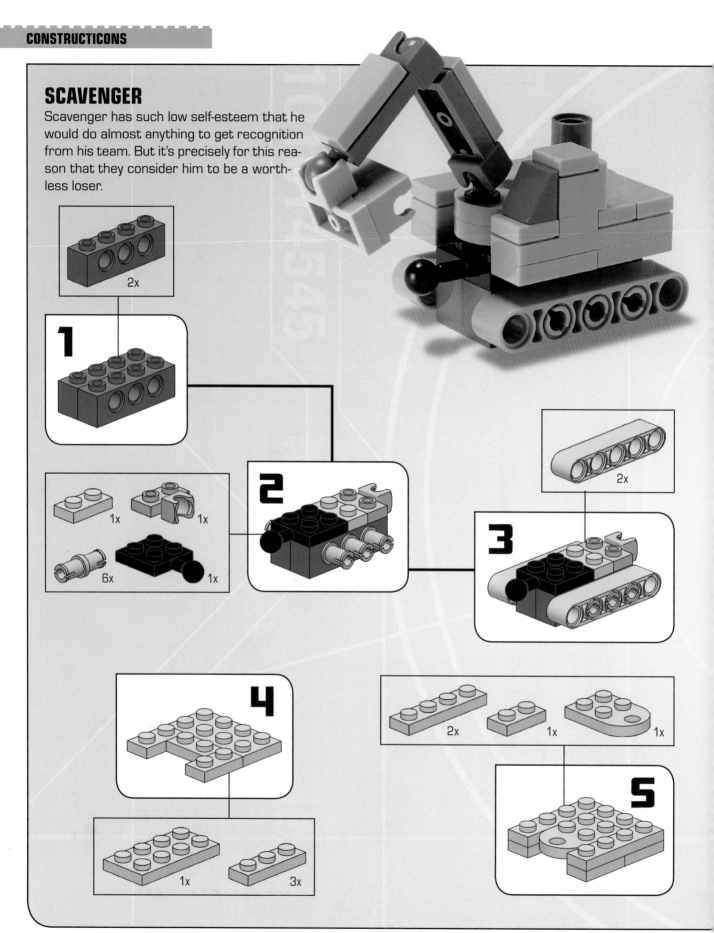

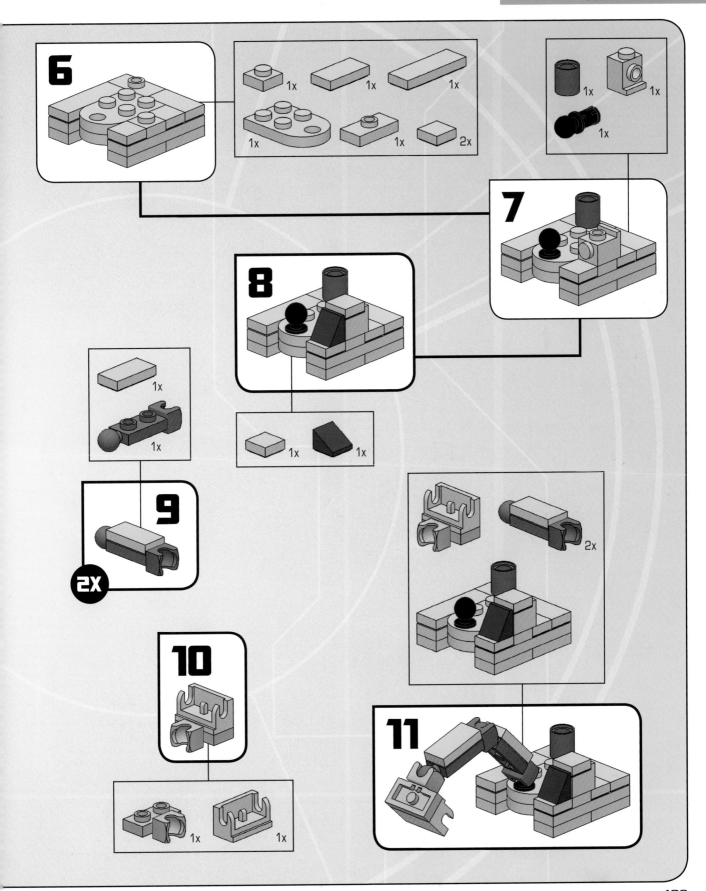

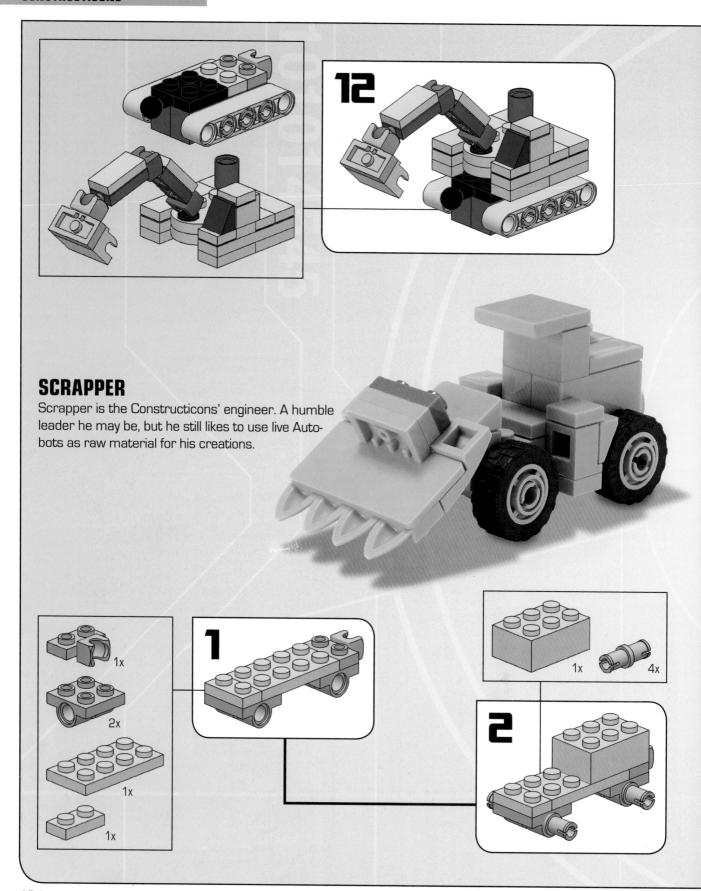

SCRAPPER

Scrapper is the Constructicons' engineer. A humble leader he may be, but he still likes to use live Auto-bots as raw material for his creations.

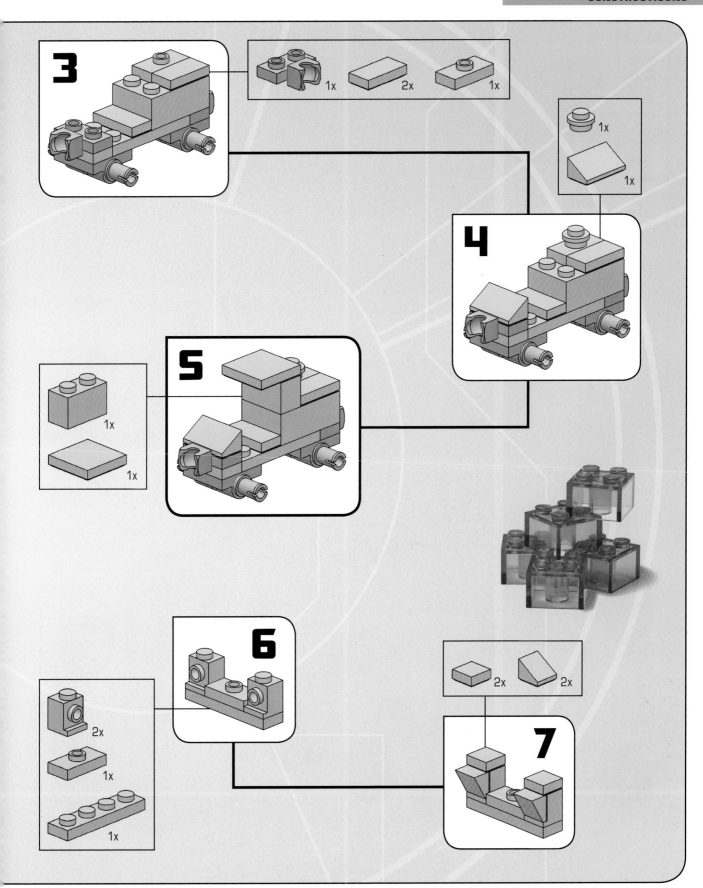

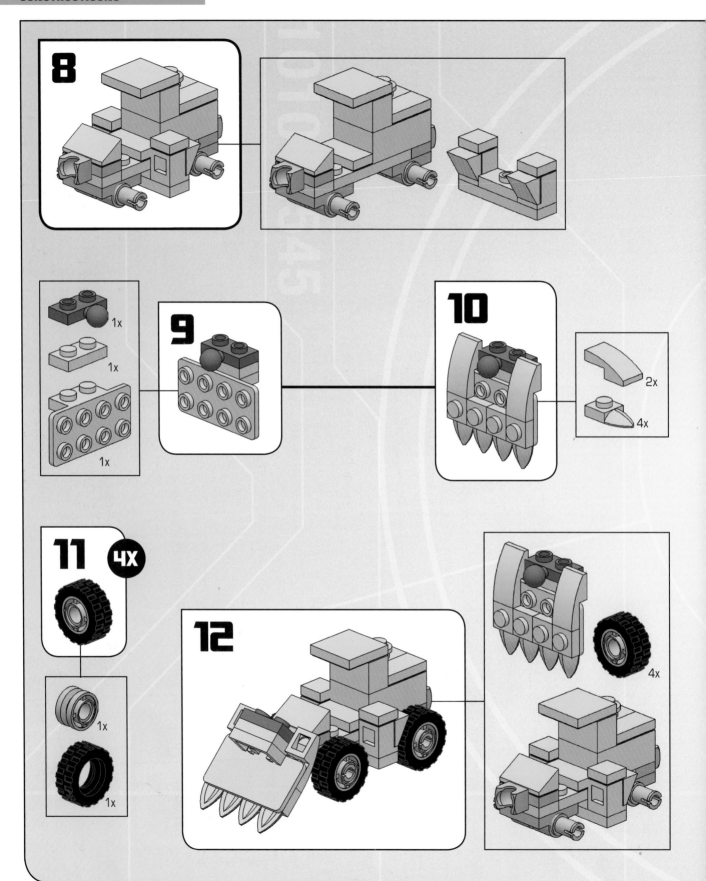

MIXMASTER

Nothing is safe from Mixmaster, whether it's materials or living robots. In Mixmaster's mixing drum everything is taken apart, processed, and transformed into almost every kind of raw material imaginable.

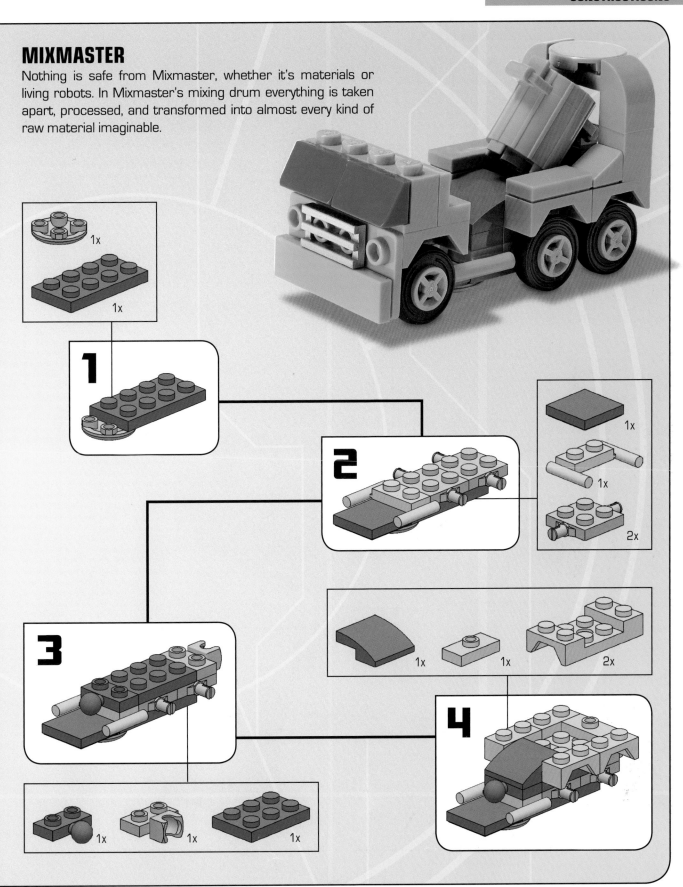

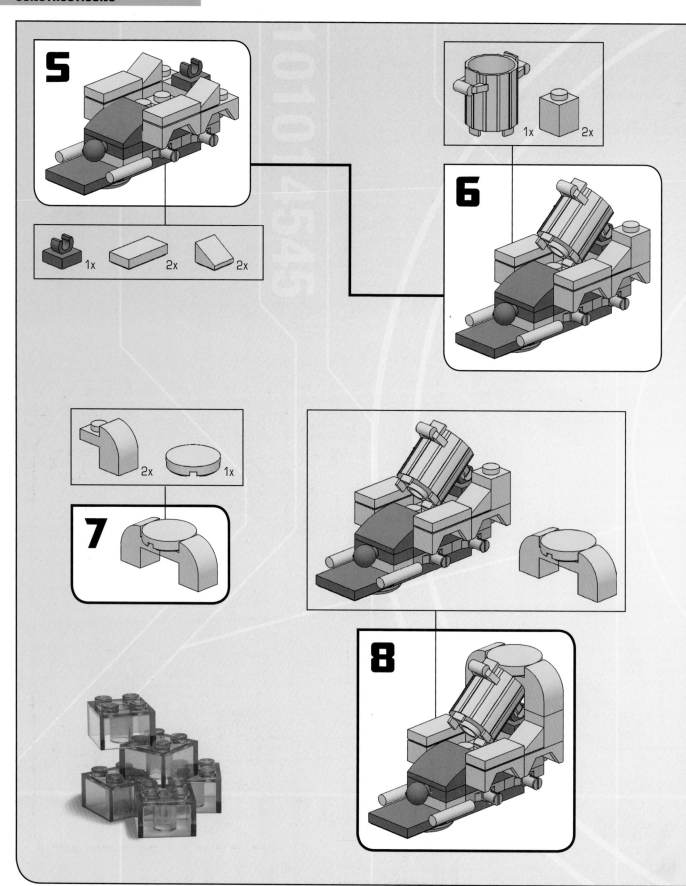

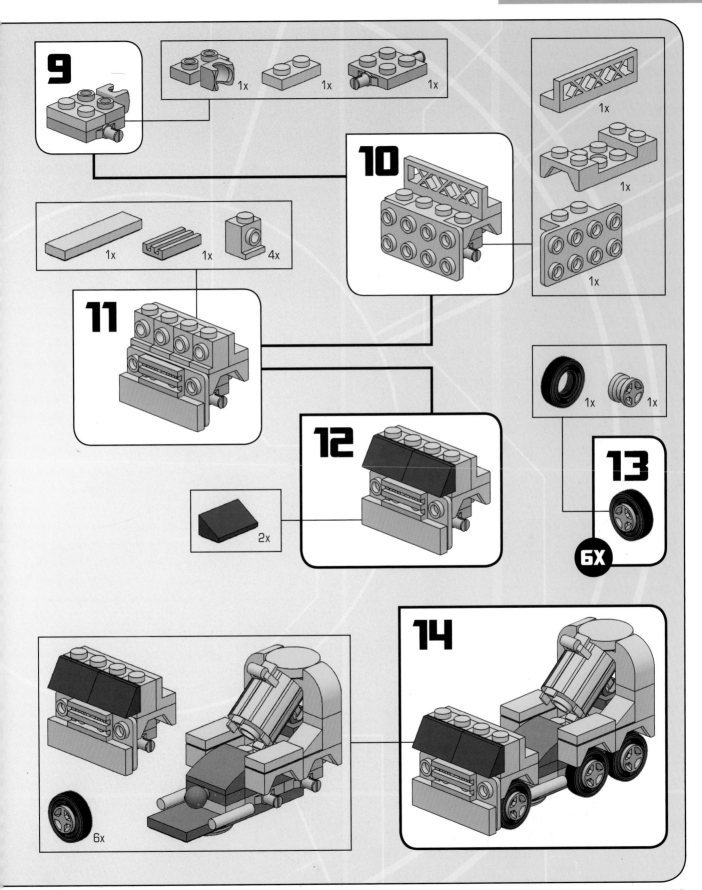

HOOK

Scrapper's Deputy is a bit of a pompous perfectionist, who likes to do even the smallest job to a T. He makes up the head and shoulders of the Devastator—something he sees as totally justified.

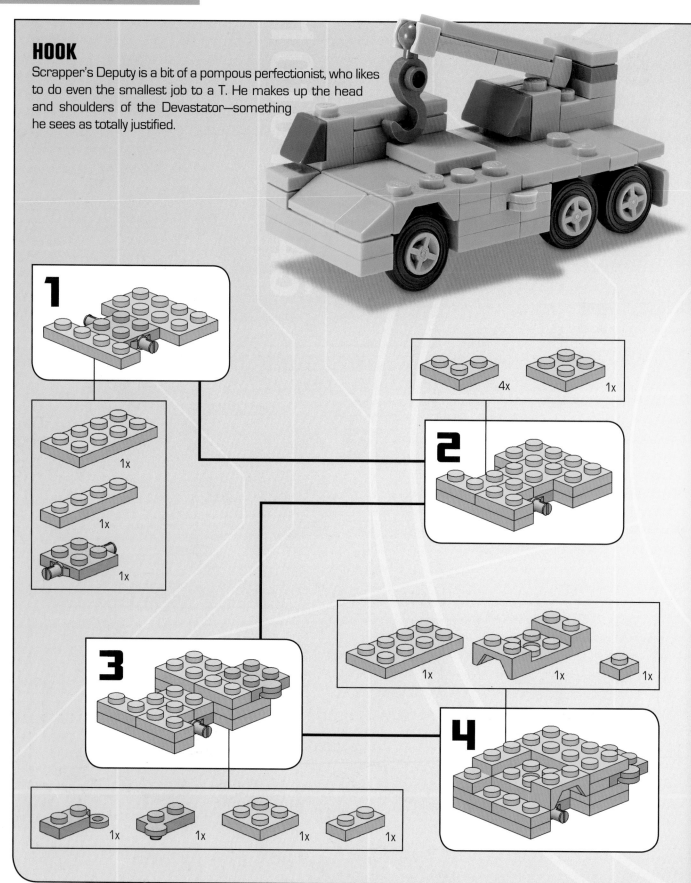

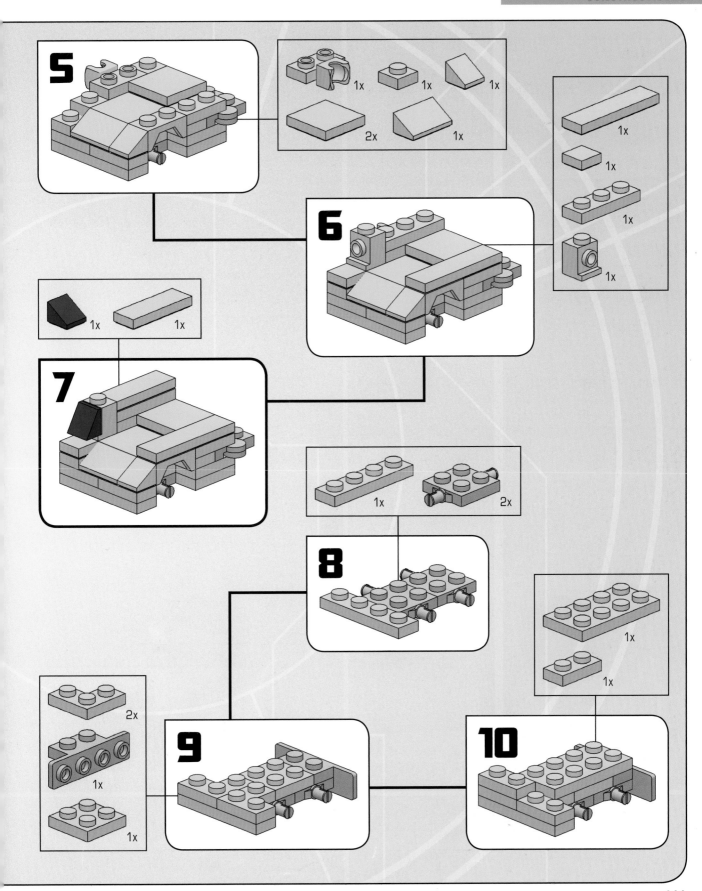

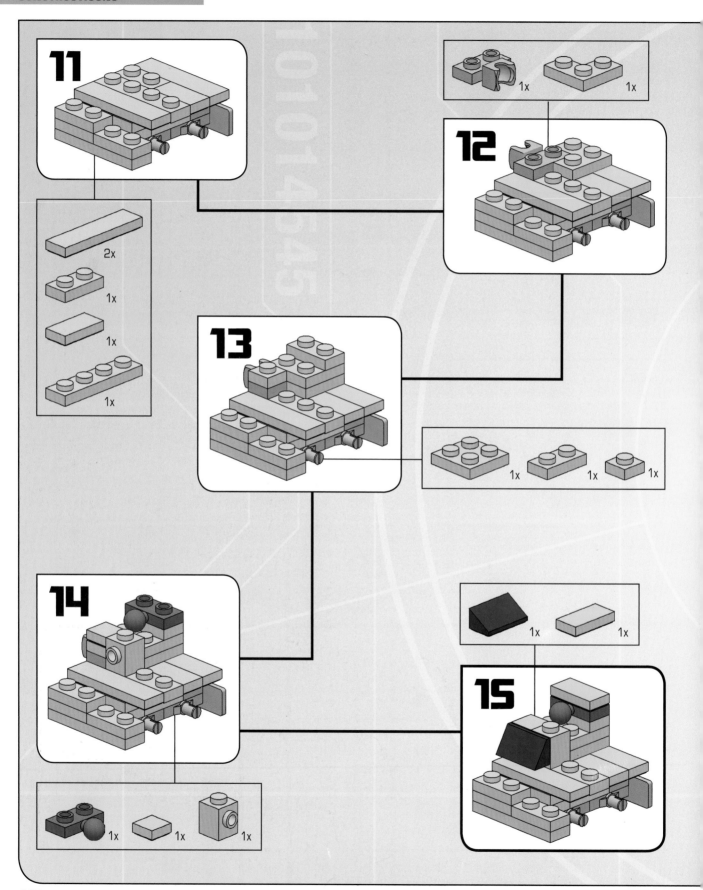

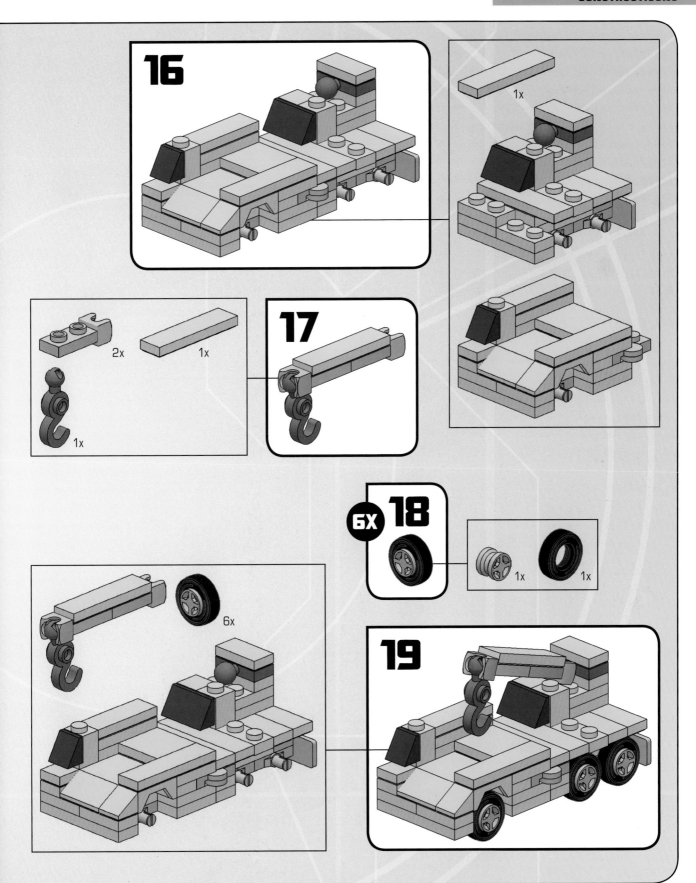

16

17

2x

1x

1x

1x

18 6X

1x 1x

6x

19

LEGS

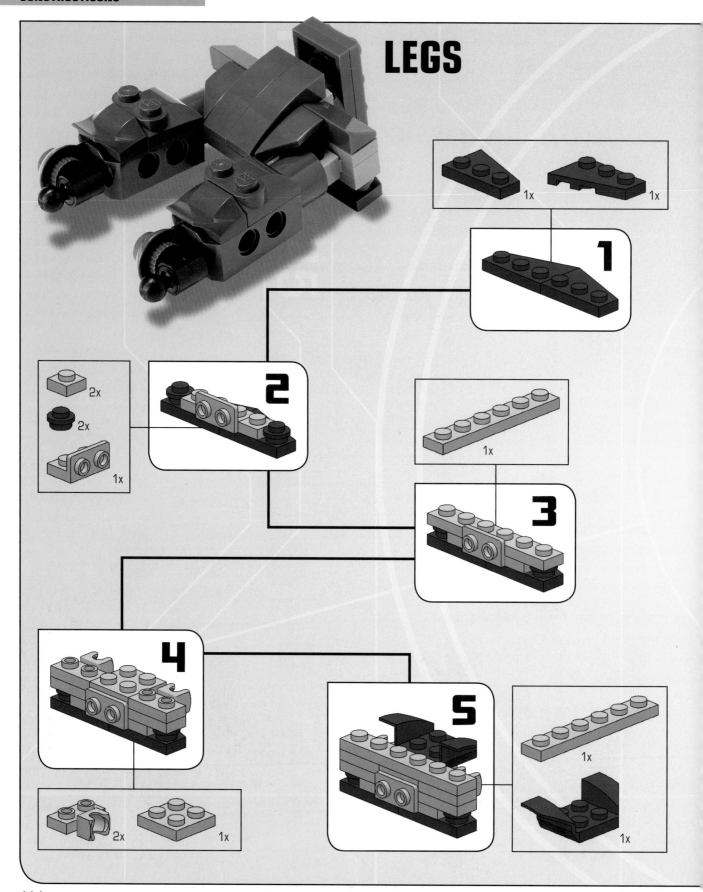

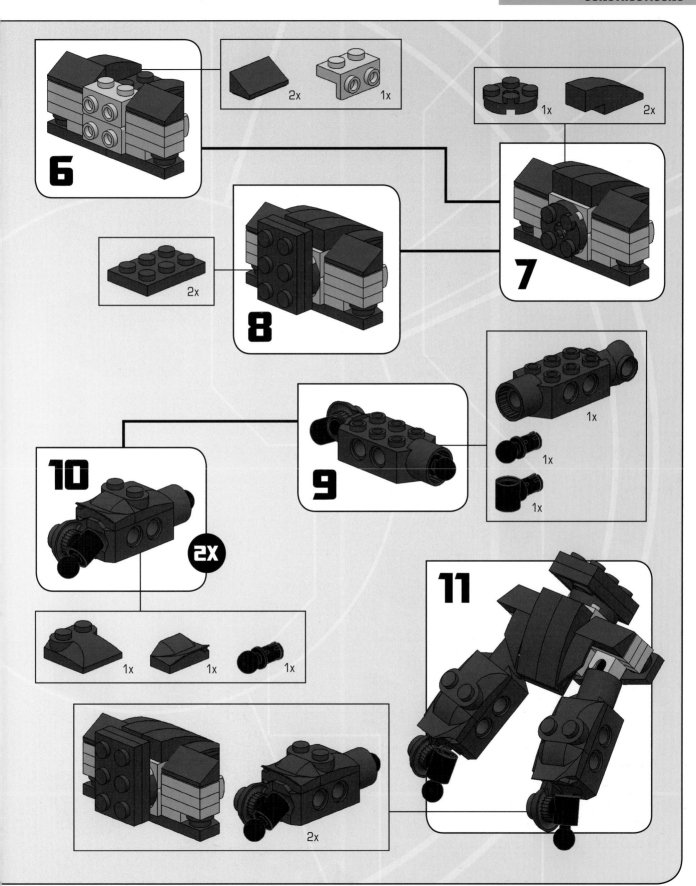

ARMS

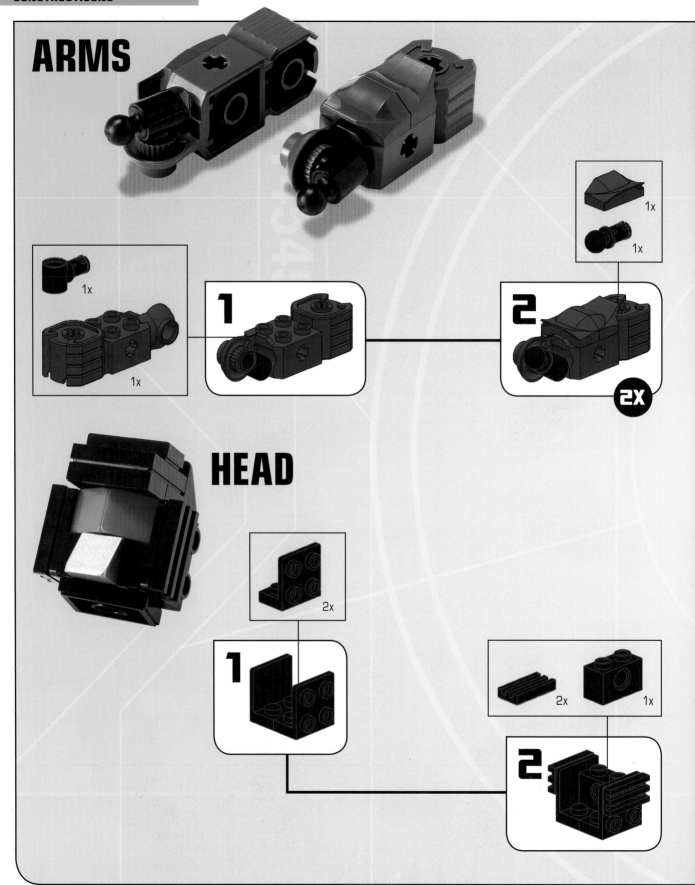

HEAD

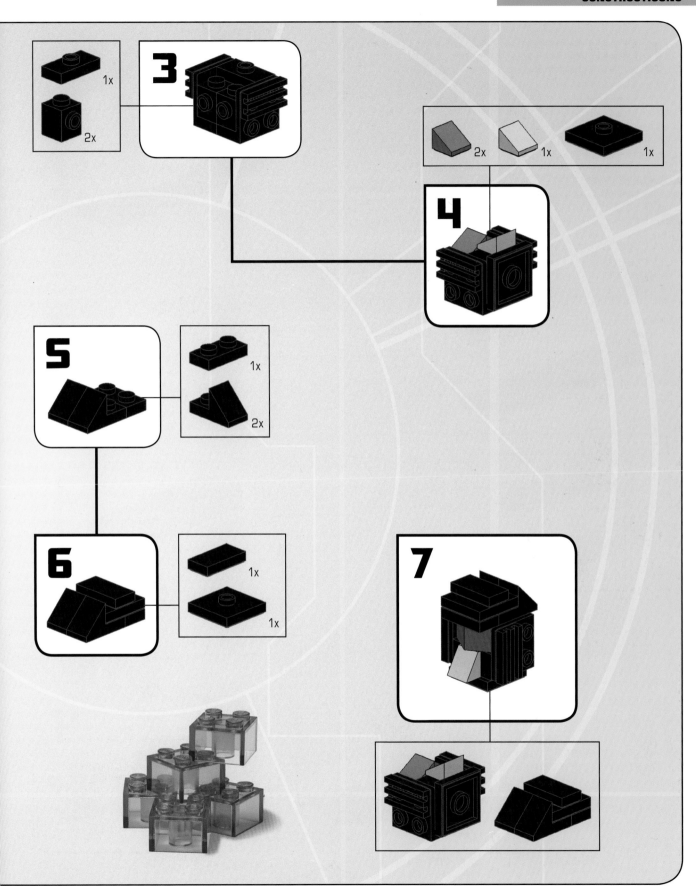

CUIRASS

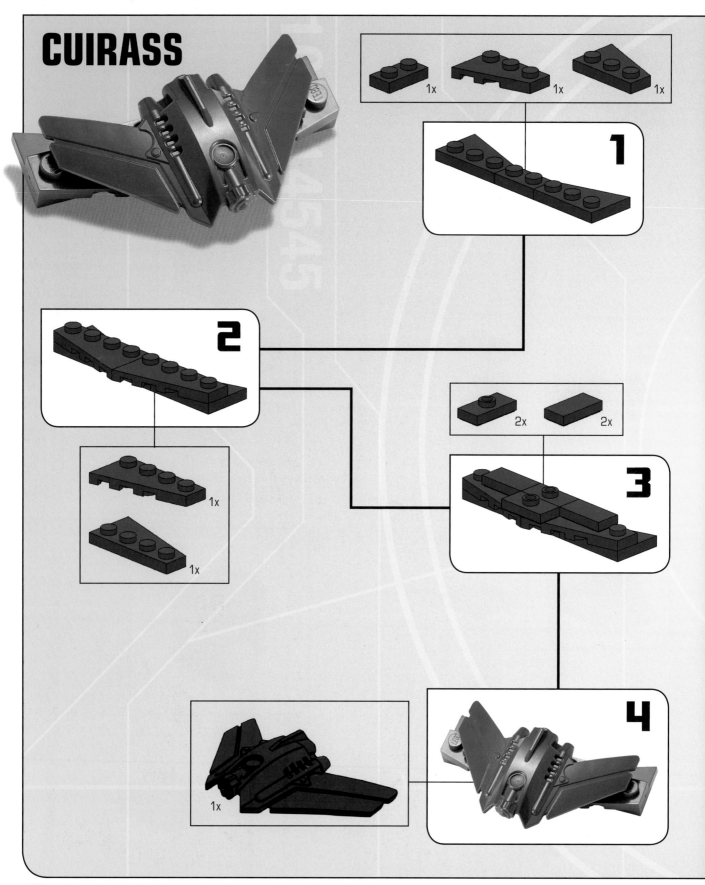

PARTS LIST

Quantity		Color	Element	Element Name	LEGO® Number
1		Light Bluish Gray	99781	Bracket 1 x 2 - 1 x 2 Down	4654582
1		Light Bluish Gray	99780	Bracket 1 x 2 - 1 x 2 Up	6004990
1		Light Bluish Gray	2436b	Bracket 1 x 2 - 1 x 4 with Rounded Corners	6014615
3		Lime	44728	Bracket 1 x 2 - 2 x 2	4569452, 6037415, 6120340
2		Black	99207	Bracket 1 x 2 - 2 x 2 Up	6000650
2		Lime	93274	Bracket 1 x 2 - 2 x 4	4617067
2		Lime	3005	Brick 1 x 1	4220634
2		Lime	3062b	Brick 1 x 1 Round with Hollow Stud	4212454
11		Lime	4070	Brick 1 x 1 with Headlight	4183879, 4540460
2		Black	87087	Brick 1 x 1 with Stud on 1 Side	4558954
1		Lime	87087	Brick 1 x 1 with Stud on 1 Side	4566860, 6073026
1		Lime	3004	Brick 1 x 2	4164022, 4613965
2		Dark Bluish Gray	30526	Brick 1 x 2 with 2 Pins	4210697
2		Lime	6091	Brick 2 x 1 x 1 & 1/3 with Curved Top	4212446
1		Lime	3003	Brick 2 x 2	4220632
1		Lime	3002	Brick 2 x 3	4220631
1		Dark Purple	41854	Car Mudguard 2 x 4 Swept Back	4566804, 6167896
4		Lime	60212	Car Mudguard 2 x 4 with Central Hole	4600186, 6121903
1		Lime	2439	Container 2 x 2 Rubbish Bin	4273737
2		Light Bluish Gray	2654	Dish 2 x 2	4211372, 4278273
1		Lime	3633	Fence Lattice 1 x 4 x 1	4618590
1		Lime	3937	Hinge 1 x 2 Base	
1		Light Bluish Gray	2429	Hinge Plate 1 x 4 Swivel Base	4219256
1		Light Bluish Gray	2430	Hinge Plate 1 x 4 Swivel Top	4219256
1		Dark Bluish Gray	30395	Hook with Towball	30395199, 4212529
2		Light Bluish Gray	3024	Plate 1 x 1	4211399
5		Lime	3024	Plate 1 x 1	4261450, 4621557
2		Dark Purple	4073	Plate 1 x 1 Round	4566522
4		Lime	4073	Plate 1 x 1 Round	4183133
1		Light Bluish Gray	85861	Plate 1 x 1 Round with Open Stud	6124825, 6168647
2		Lime	4081b	Plate 1 x 1 with Clip Light Type 2	4558600, 4632576
4		Lime	49668	Plate 1 x 1 with Tooth In-line	4611784
1		Black	3023	Plate 1 x 2	302326
1		Dark Purple	3023	Plate 1 x 2	4224858, 4655695

Quantity		Color	Element	Element Name	LEGO® Number
18		Lime	3023	Plate 1 x 2	4164037
5		Dark Bluish Gray	14417	Plate 1 x 2 with Ball Joint-8	6039479
2		Dark Purple	15573	Plate 1 x 2 with Groove with 1 Centre Stud, without Understud	6092604
4		Lime	3839b	Plate 1 x 2 with Handles Type 2	4168244
2		Light Bluish Gray	14418	Plate 1 x 2 with Socket Joint-8 with Friction	6043639
2		Dark Bluish Gray	14419	Plate 1 x 2 with Socket Joint-8 with Friction and Ball Joint-8	6039482
11		Light Bluish Gray	14704	Plate 1 x 2 with Socket Joint-8 with Friction Centre	6043656
1		Lime	14704	Plate 1 x 2 with Socket Joint-8 with Friction Centre	
1		Black	3794a	Plate 1 x 2 without Groove with 1 Centre Stud	
6		Lime	3794a	Plate 1 x 2 without Groove with 1 Centre Stud	
1		Lime	3623	Plate 1 x 3	4210210
7		Lime	3710	Plate 1 x 4	4187743
2		Light Bluish Gray	3666	Plate 1 x 6	4211438
1		Light Bluish Gray	3022	Plate 2 x 2	4211397
8		Lime	3022	Plate 2 x 2	4203892, 4537937, 4613977
7		Lime	2420	Plate 2 x 2 Corner	4210207, 4633822
1		Dark Purple	4032b	Plate 2 x 2 Round with Axlehole Type 2	
2		Black	87580	Plate 2 x 2 with Groove with 1 Center Stud	4565323
2		Light Bluish Gray	2817	Plate 2 x 2 with Holes	4211376
2		Black	15456	Plate 2 x 2 with Towball and Centre Hole	6051038
8		Light Bluish Gray	4600	Plate 2 x 2 with Wheel Holders	4211504
1		Dark Bluish Gray	3021	Plate 2 x 3	4211043
3		Dark Purple	3021	Plate 2 x 3	4225142
1		Lime	3021	Plate 2 x 3	4210215, 4534666, 6013530
1		Dark Bluish Gray	3020	Plate 2 x 4	4211065
7		Lime	3020	Plate 2 x 4	4164023, 4534667, 4537936
2		Lime	3176	Plate 3 x 2 with Hole	6175325
2		Lime	61409	Slope Brick 18 2 x 1 x 2/3 Grille	4521216, 4540385
3		Dark Purple	54200	Slope Brick 31 1 x 1 x 0.667	4255409, 4567509
6		Lime	54200	Slope Brick 31 1 x 1 x 0.667	4298015, 4504372

Quantity		Color	Element	Element Name	LEGO® Number
1		Metallic Silver	54200	Slope Brick 31 1 x 1 x 0.667	4528609, 6092109
2		Red	54200	Slope Brick 31 1 x 1 x 0.667	4244371, 4504379, 5074621
5		Dark Purple	85984	Slope Brick 31 1 x 2 x 0.667	4566607
4		Lime	85984	Slope Brick 31 1 x 2 x 0.667	6025026
2		Lime	3040	Slope Brick 45 2 x 1	4537925
6		Dark Purple	47458	Slope Brick Curved 1 x 2 x 2/3 with Fin without Studs	
2		Lime	11477	Slope Brick Curved 2 x 1	6069006
2		Dark Purple	47457	Slope Brick Curved 2 x 2 x 2/3 Triple with Two Top Studs	4218700, 4579024, 6109766
1		Dark Bluish Gray	15068	Slope Brick Curved 2 x 2 x 0.667	6071261
2		Dark Purple	50950	Slope Brick Curved 3 x 1	4578772, 6103449
2		Black	92946	Slope Plate 45 2 x 1	4653087, 6069000
2		Dark Bluish Gray	18654	Technic Beam 1	6100030
4		Lime	32316	Technic Beam 5	4265700, 4571220, 4661486
1		Black	3700	Technic Brick 1 x 2 with Hole	370026
2		Dark Bluish Gray	3701	Technic Brick 1 x 4 with Holes	4213607
2		Dark Purple	47431	Technic Brick 2 x 2 w/ Axlehole, Click Rot. Hinge (V) and Fist	4218235
2		Dark Purple	47432	Technic Brick 2 x 3 w/ Holes, Click Rot. Hinge (V) and Socket	4218091
10		Light Bluish Gray	3673	Technic Pin	3673194, 4211807
1		Light Bluish Gray	4274	Technic Pin 1/2	4211483, 4274194
7		Black	6628	Technic Pin Towball with Friction	4184169, 662826
4		Black	15100	Technic Pin with Friction with Perpendicular Pin Hole	6073231
1		Dark Bluish Gray	15712	Tile 1 x 1 with Clip (Thick C-Clip)	6071226
10		Lime	3070b	Tile 1 x 1 with Groove	4537251
2		Black	2412b	Tile 1 x 2 Grille with Groove	241226
1		Metallic Silver	2412b	Tile 1 x 2 Grille with Groove	4249040, 51815301, 6051422
1		Black	3069b	Tile 1 x 2 with Groove	306926
2		Dark Purple	3069b	Tile 1 x 2 with Groove	4613192
12		Lime	3069b	Tile 1 x 2 with Groove	4164025, 4500125
2		Lime	63864	Tile 1 x 3 with Groove	4565993

Quantity	Color		Element	Element Name	LEGO® Number
6		Lime	2431	Tile 1 x 4 with Groove	4164021
1		Lime	4150	Tile 2 x 2 Round with Cross Underside Stud	4541957
1		Dark Bluish Gray	3068b	Tile 2 x 2 with Groove	4211055
6		Lime	3068b	Tile 2 x 2 with Groove	4518611
12		Black	59895	Tyre 4/ 80 x 8 Single Smooth Type 2	4516843
4		Black	92409	Tyre 6.4/ 75 x 8 Shallow Offset Tread with Centre Band	4617848
4		Black	4084	Tyre 8/ 75 x 8 Offset Tread	
16		Light Bluish Gray	4624	Wheel Rim 6.4 x 8	4211506
4		Light Bluish Gray	42610	Wheel Rim 8 x 11.2 with Centre Groove	4211758
2		Dark Purple	43723	Wing 2 x 3 Left	4616558
1		Lime	43723	Wing 2 x 3 Left	4183168, 4539907
2		Dark Purple	43722	Wing 2 x 3 Right	4616557
1		Lime	43722	Wing 2 x 3 Right	4183167, 4539908
1		Lime	51739	Wing 2 x 4	6025027
1		Dark Purple	41770	Wing 2 x 4 Left	4225170
1		Lime	41770	Wing 2 x 4 Left	4164034
1		Dark Purple	41769	Wing 2 x 4 Right	4225145
1		Lime	41769	Wing 2 x 4 Right	4164033
1		Dark Purple	89589	Hero Factory Shoulder Armor with Wing	6001498

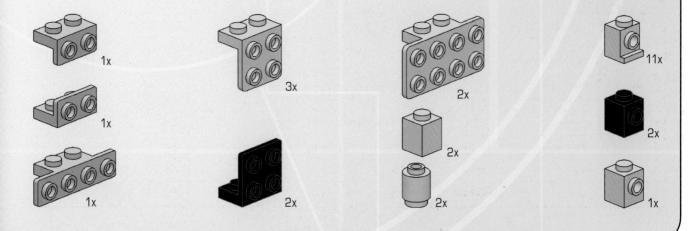

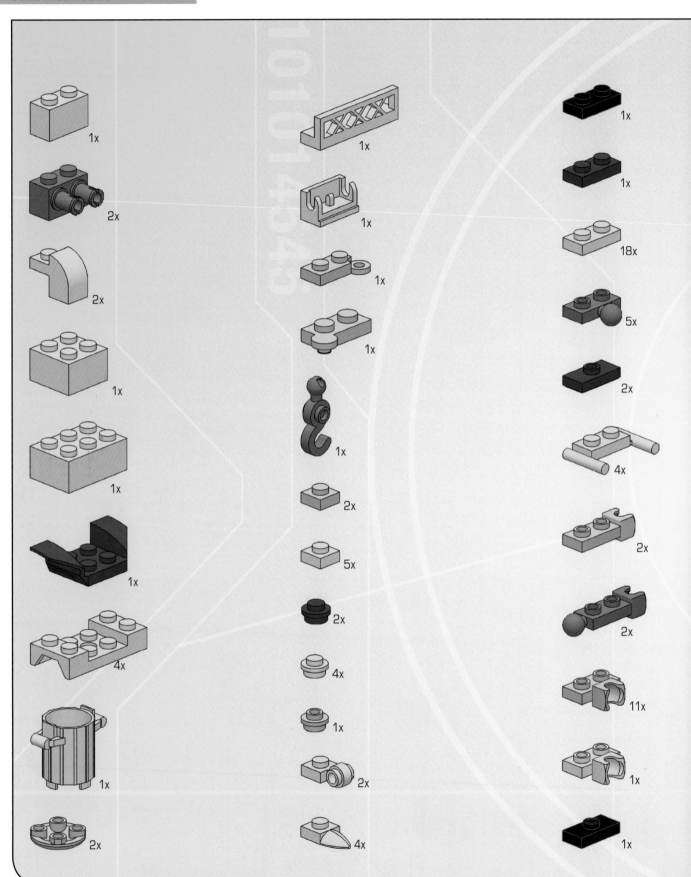

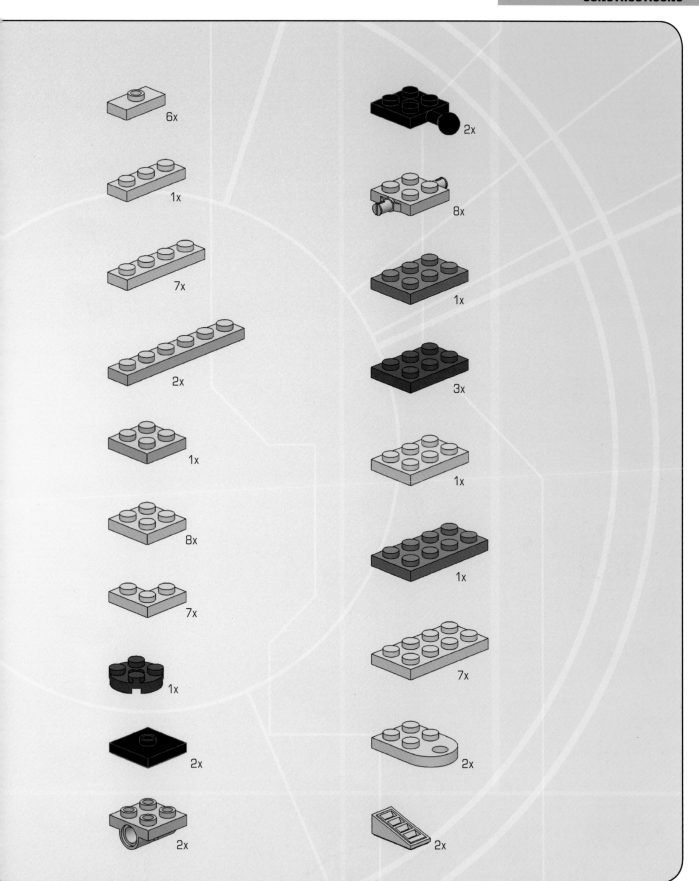

6x

1x

7x

2x

1x

8x

7x

1x

2x

2x

2x

8x

1x

3x

1x

1x

7x

2x

2x

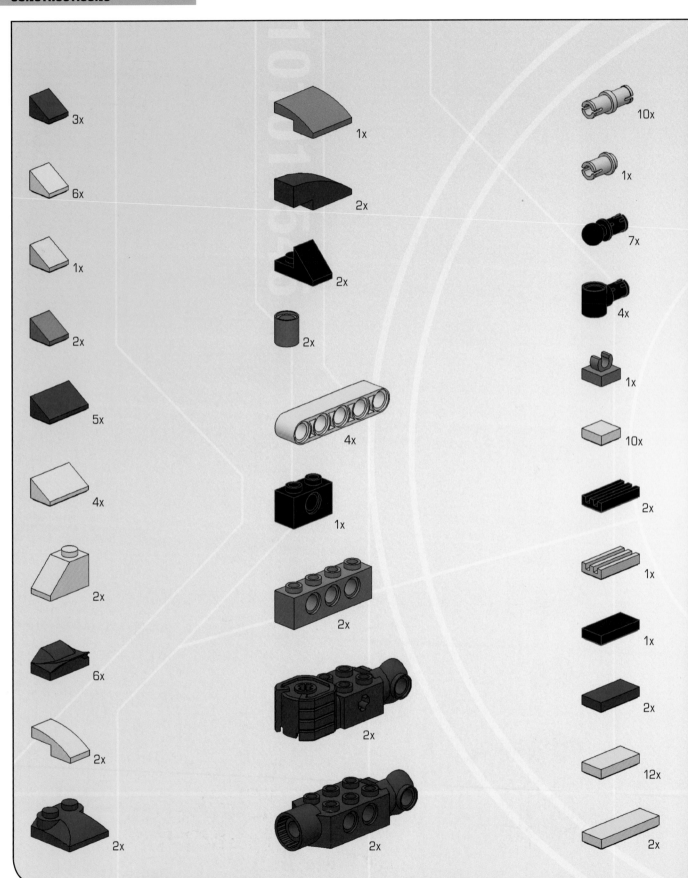

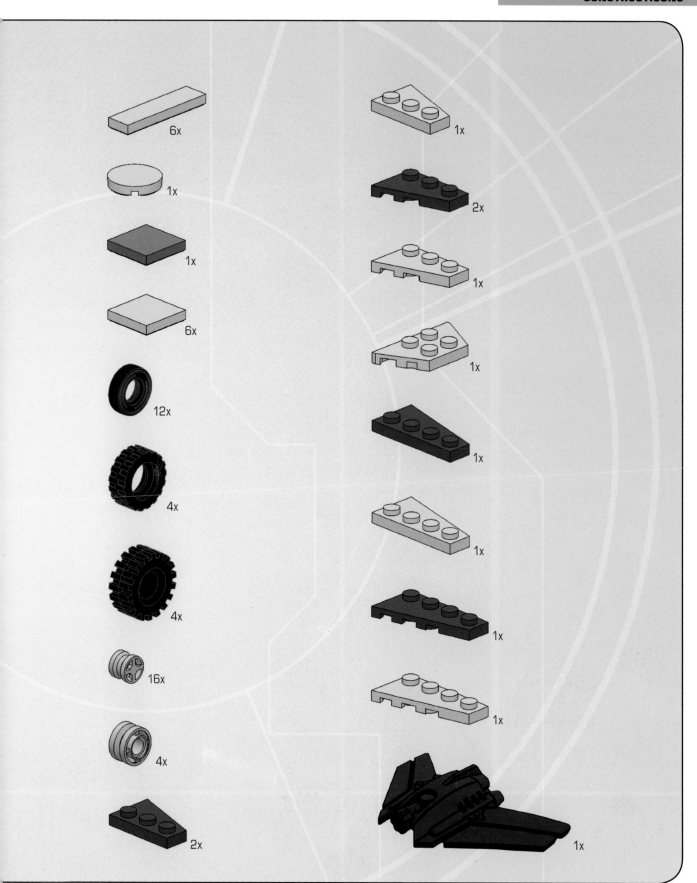

6x

1x

1x

2x

1x

6x

1x

12x

1x

4x

1x

4x

1x

16x

1x

4x

1x

2x

1x

OPTIMUS PRIME

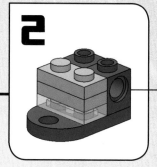

As leader of the Autobots, Optimus Prime is one of the strongest in the team. He bears the Matrix of Leadership on his chest, which gives him extra energy. Here you have the option to build Optimus in gray or get some of the rare old chrome parts to make the model more authentic.

This model consists of approximately 800 parts and takes the form of a truck that is a maximum 10 studs wide. It's very important for me to get the proportions for Altmode and Botmode just right so that they work together. The transformation is simple, but it's important to remember to use the specially designed element to stabilize the hips in the robot shape. Otherwise the torso could tilt backward.

Optimus Prime's arsenal includes a laser gun and an energon-ax; you can see exploded-view pictures as building instructions for them on the following pages.

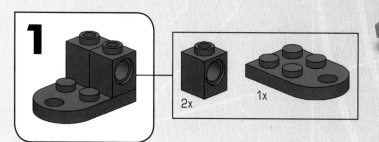

1

2x   1x

2

1x   2x

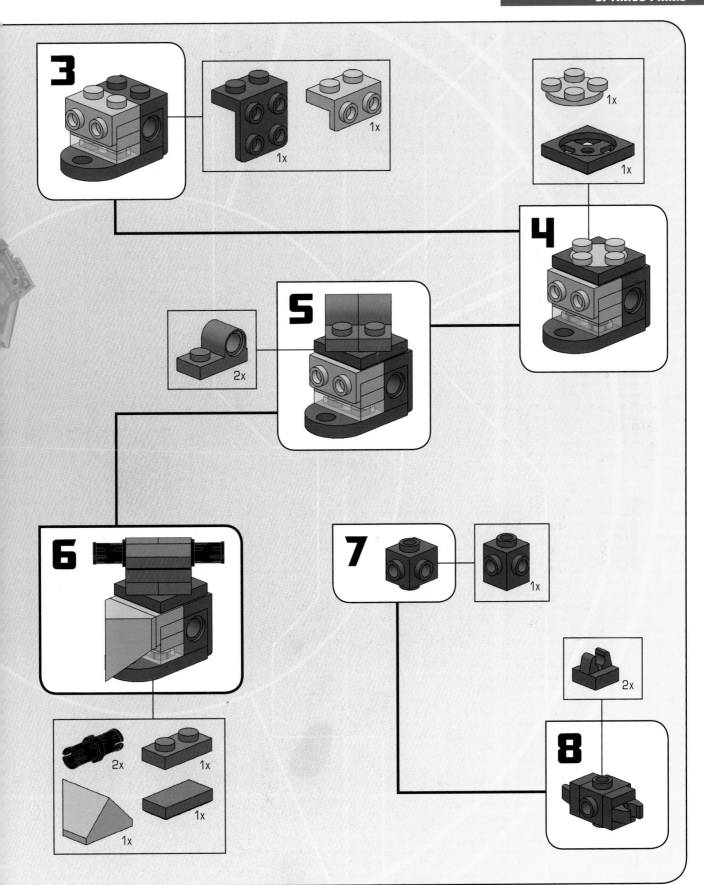

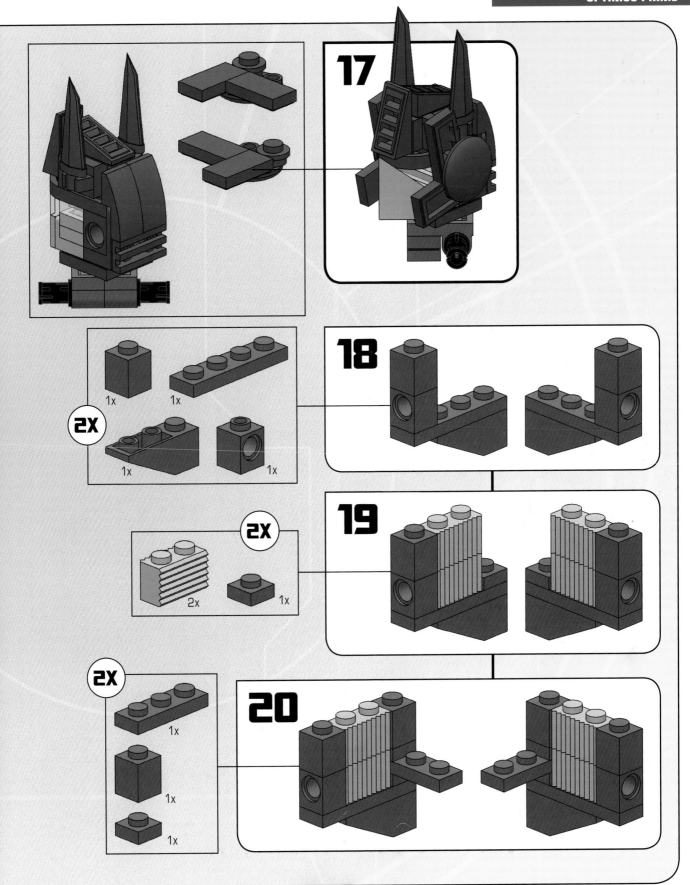

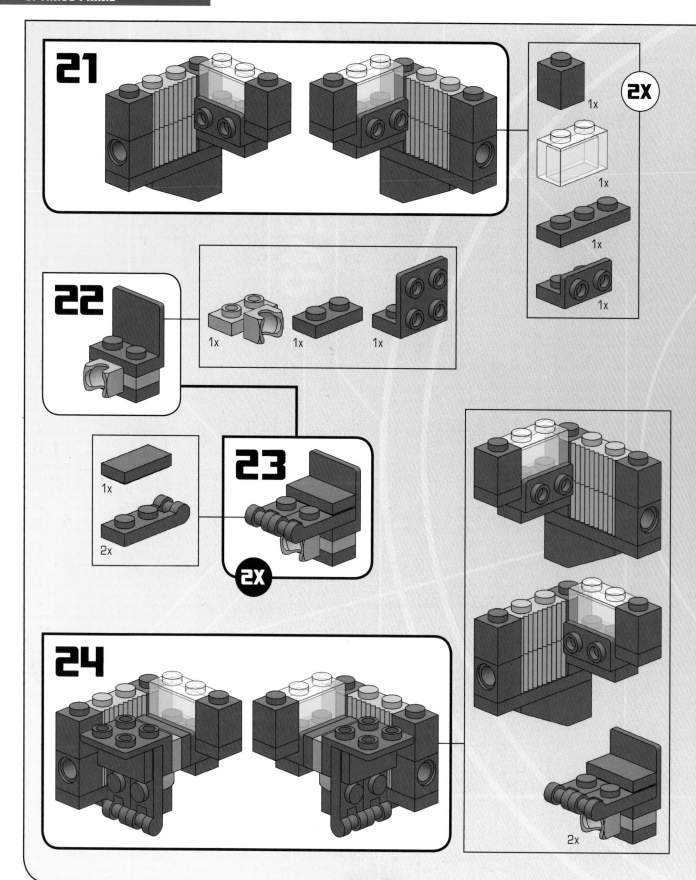

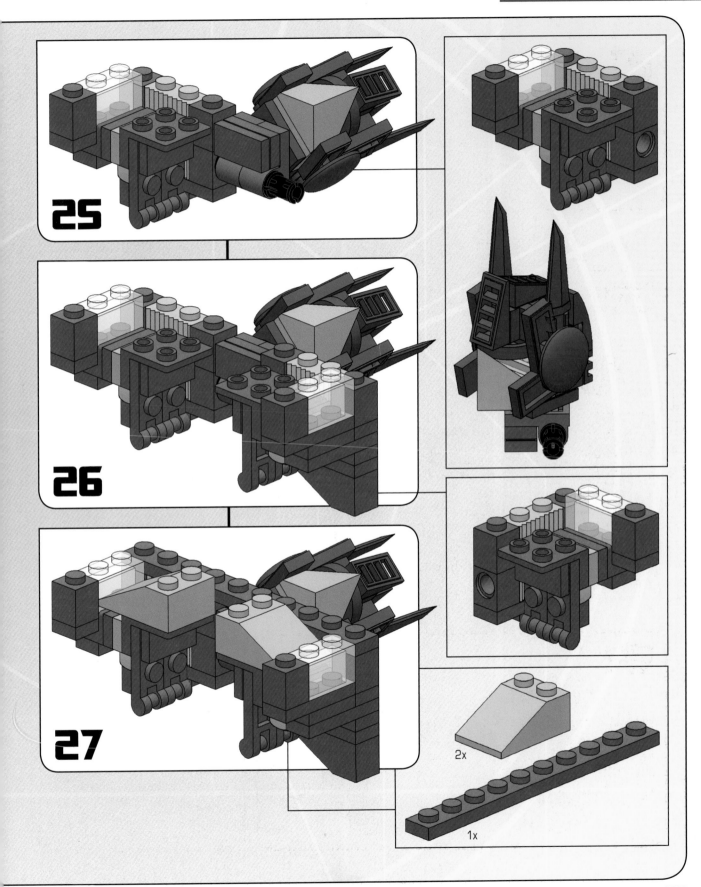

25

26

27

2x

1x

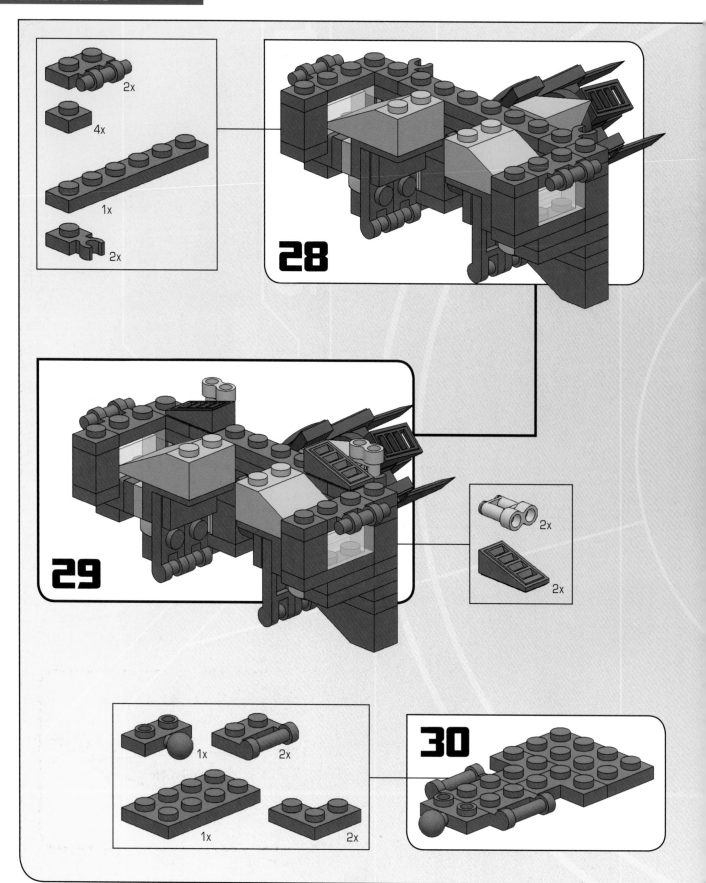

28

2x
4x
1x
2x

29

2x
2x

30

1x
2x
1x
2x

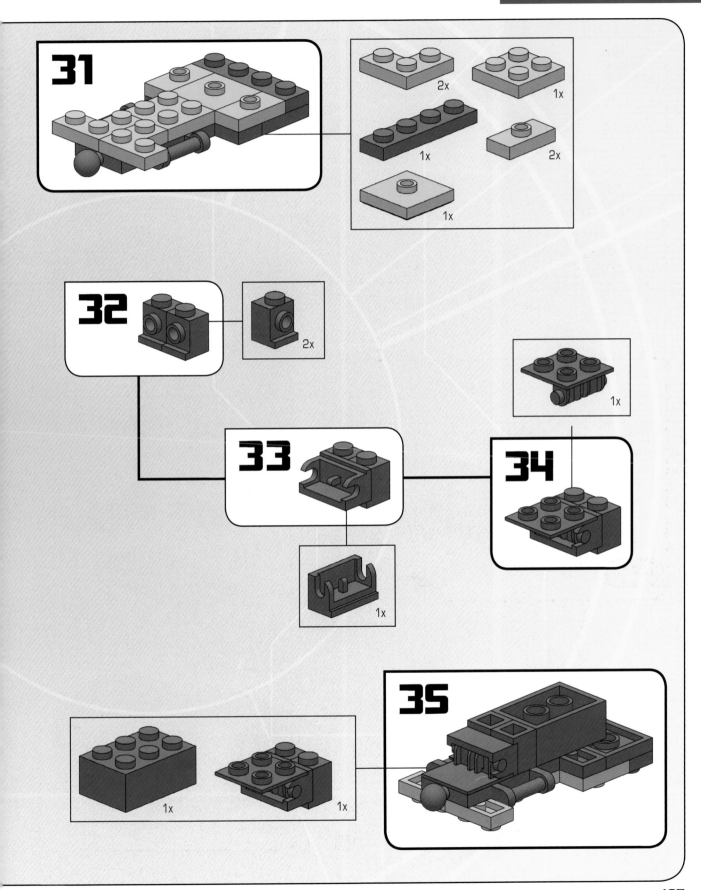

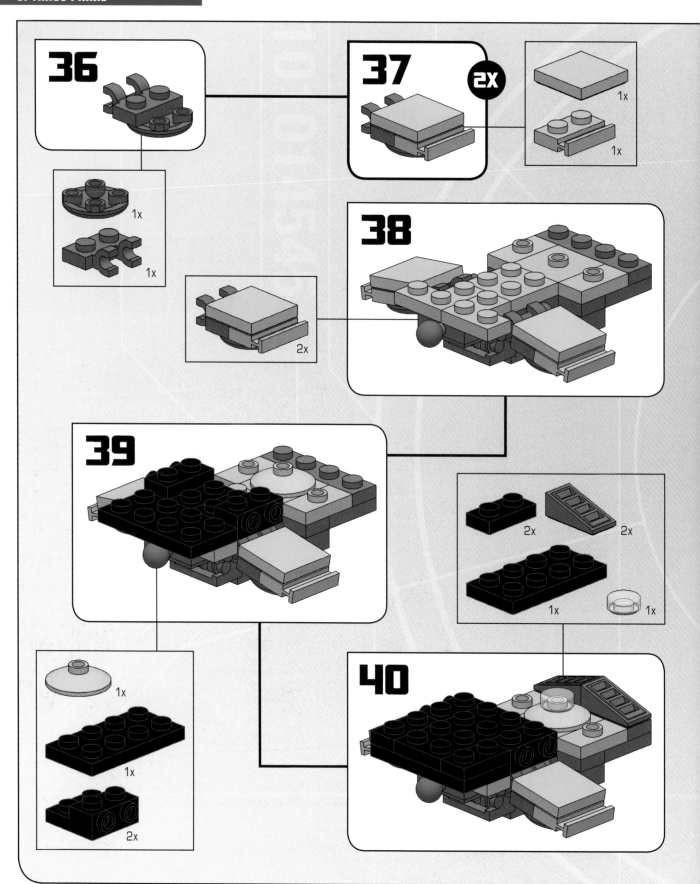

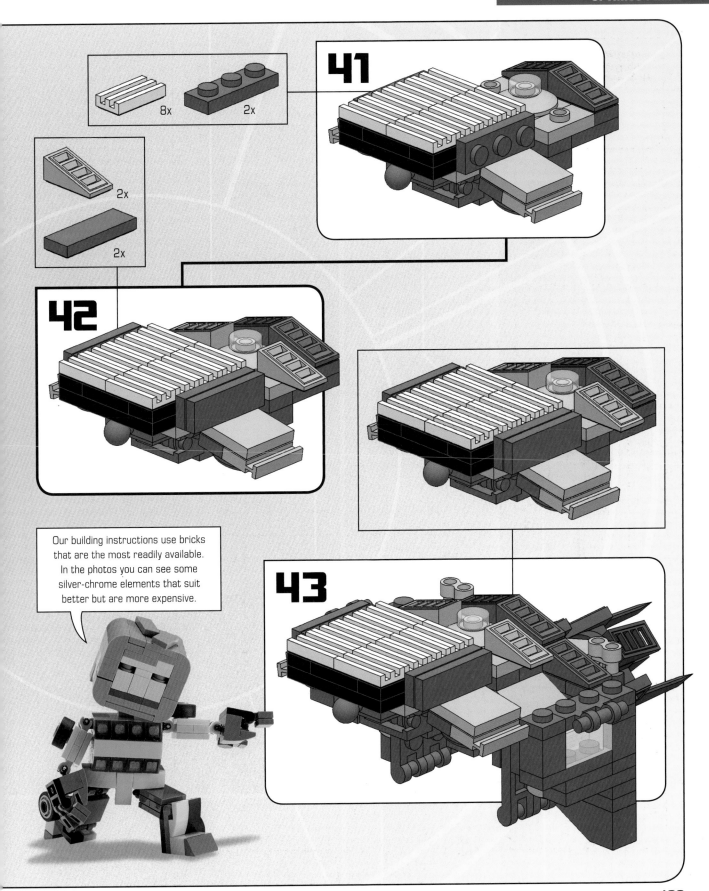

41

8x   2x

2x

2x

42

Our building instructions use bricks that are the most readily available. In the photos you can see some silver-chrome elements that suit better but are more expensive.

43

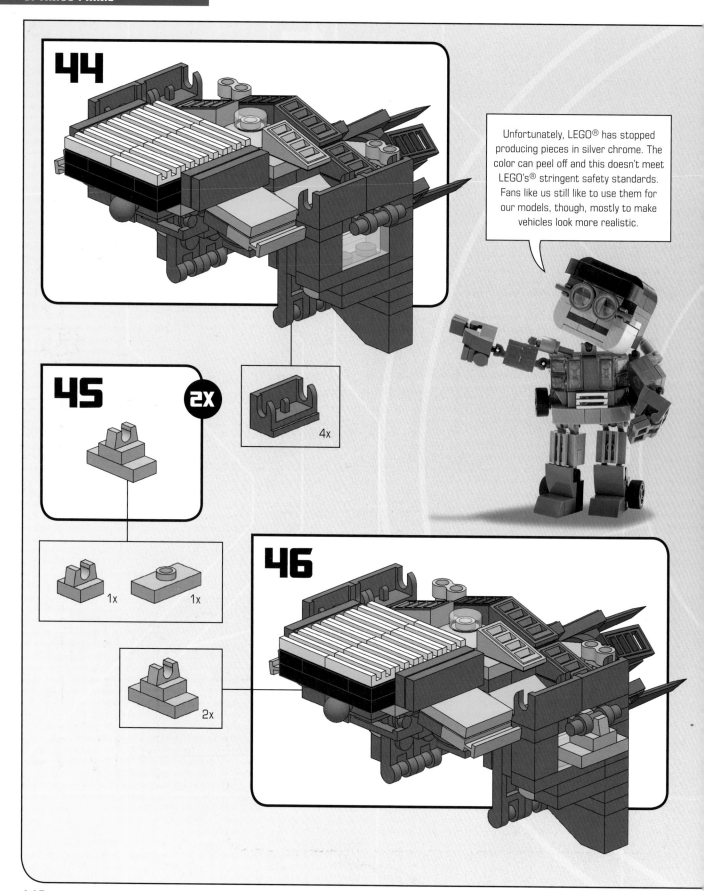

44

Unfortunately, LEGO® has stopped producing pieces in silver chrome. The color can peel off and this doesn't meet LEGO's® stringent safety standards. Fans like us still like to use them for our models, though, mostly to make vehicles look more realistic.

45 2X

4x

1x 1x

46

2x

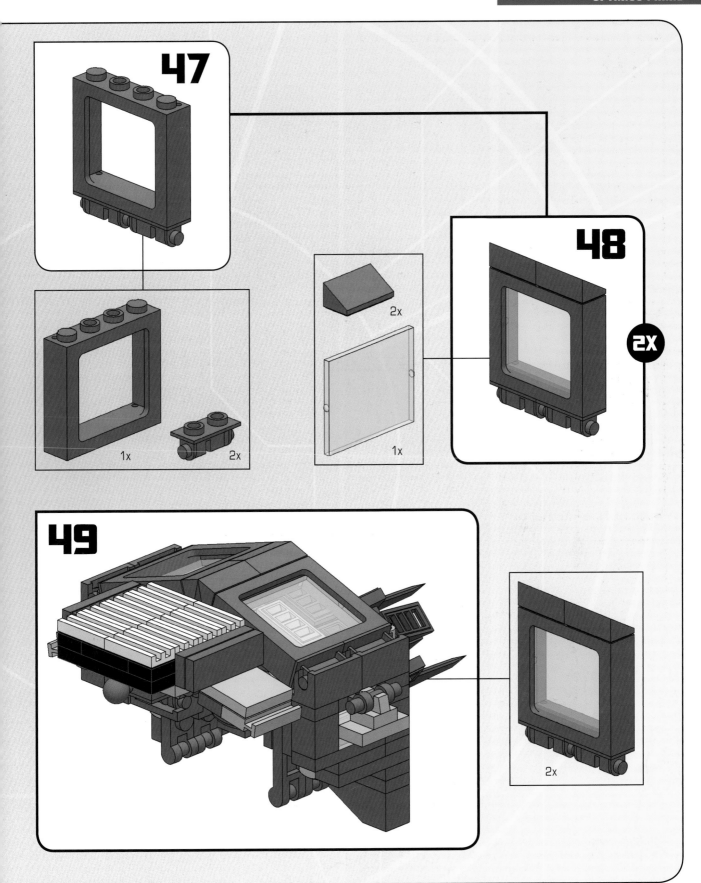

50

2x 2x 1x

51

2x

52

This element is a built
2 x 4-Module that is fixed onto
the hips in Botmode.

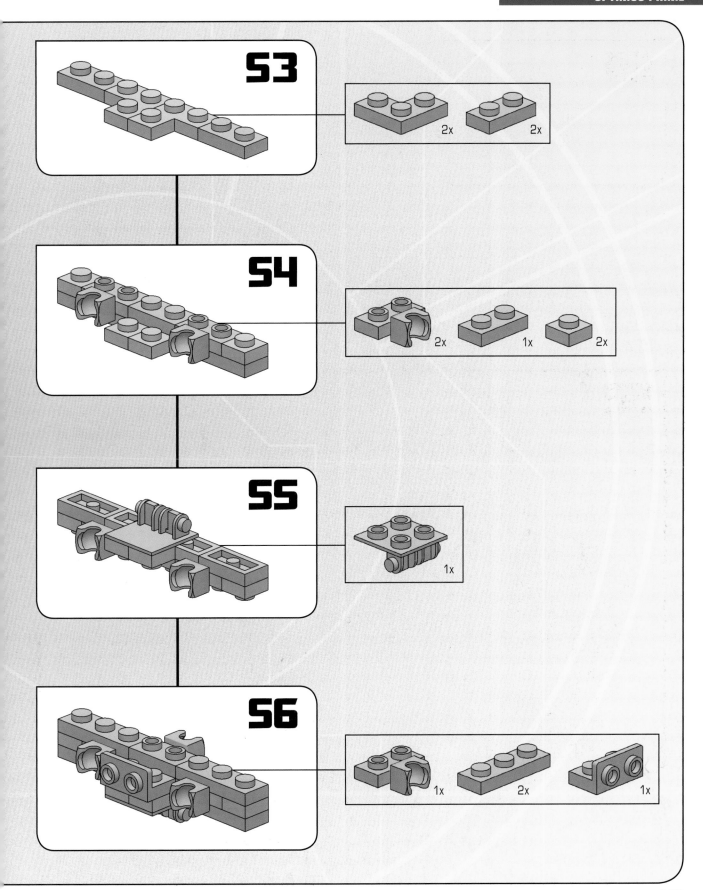

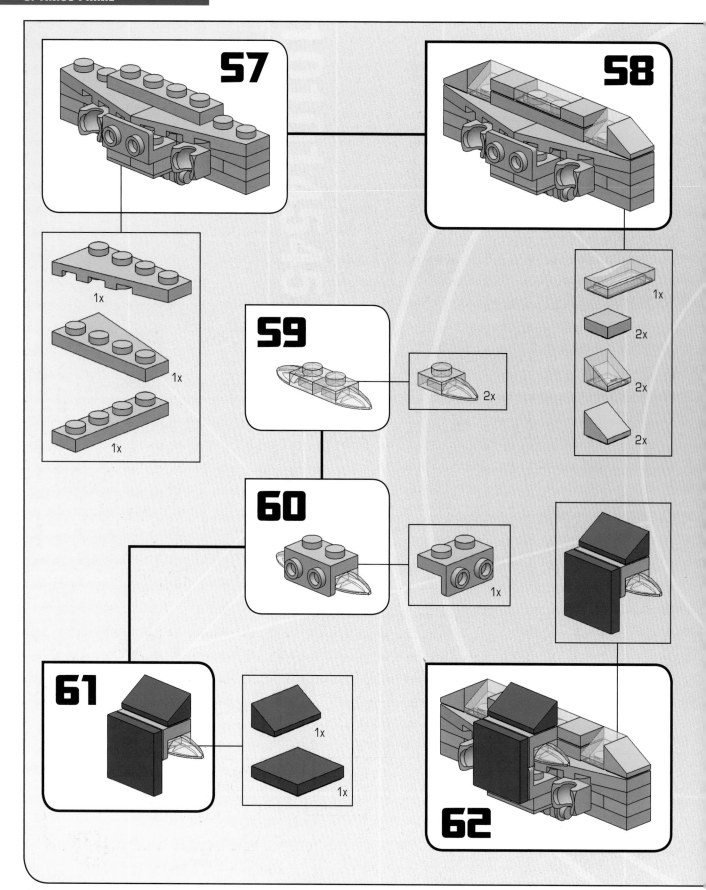

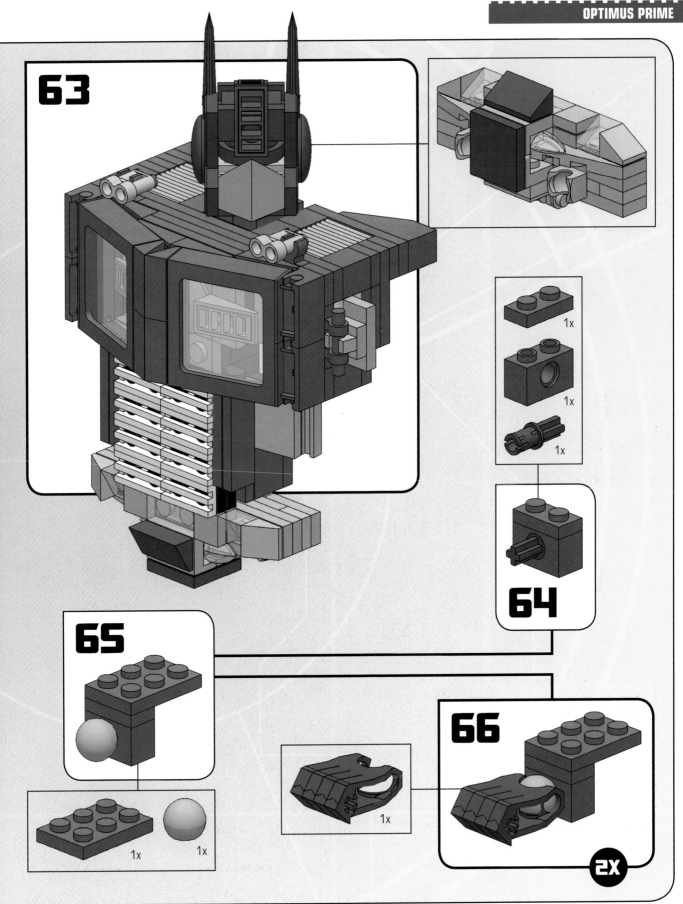

63

64

65

1x
1x

66

1x

2X

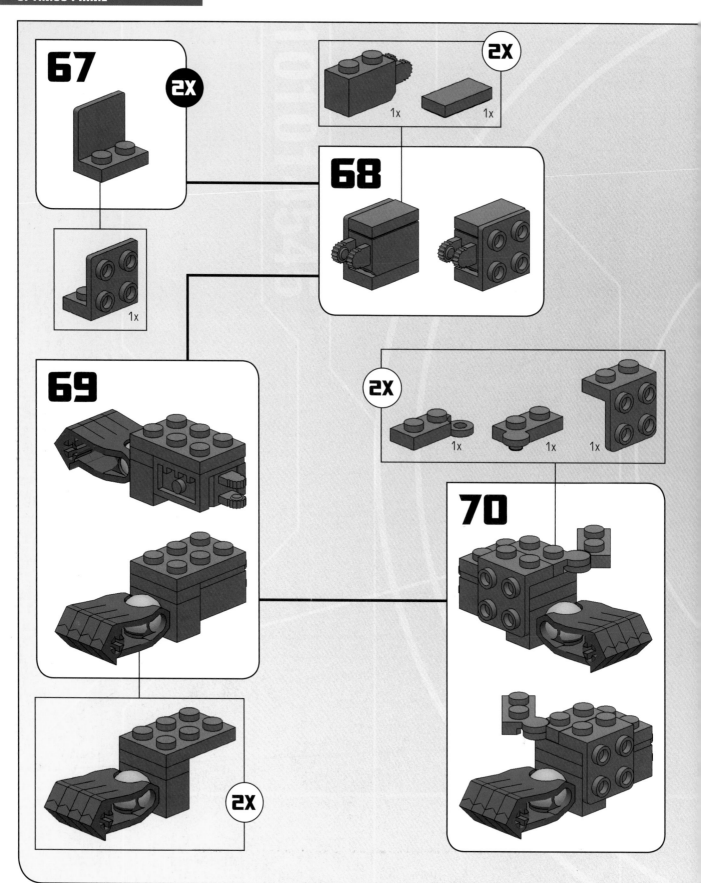

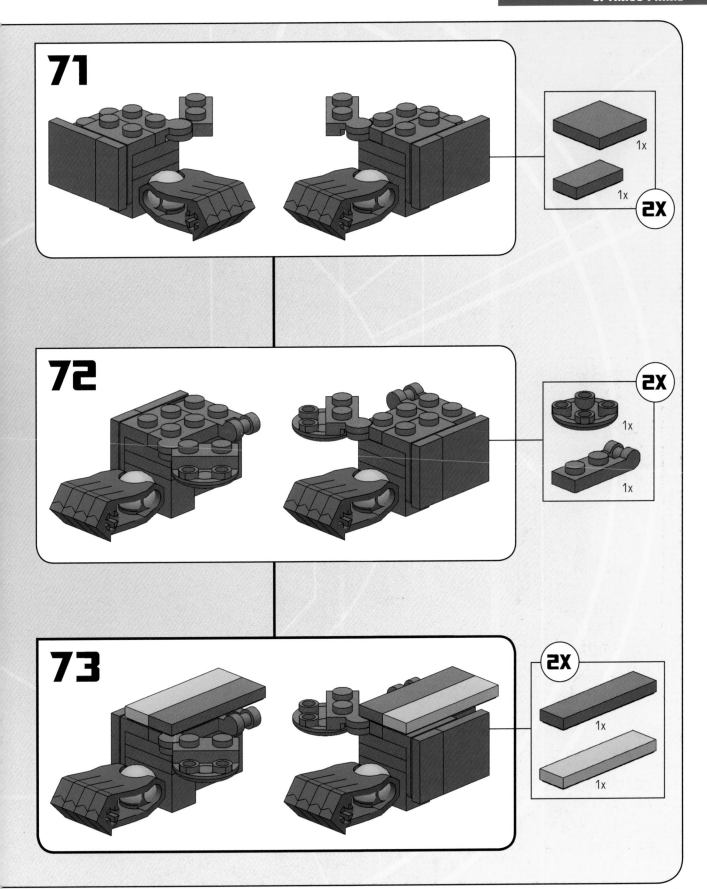

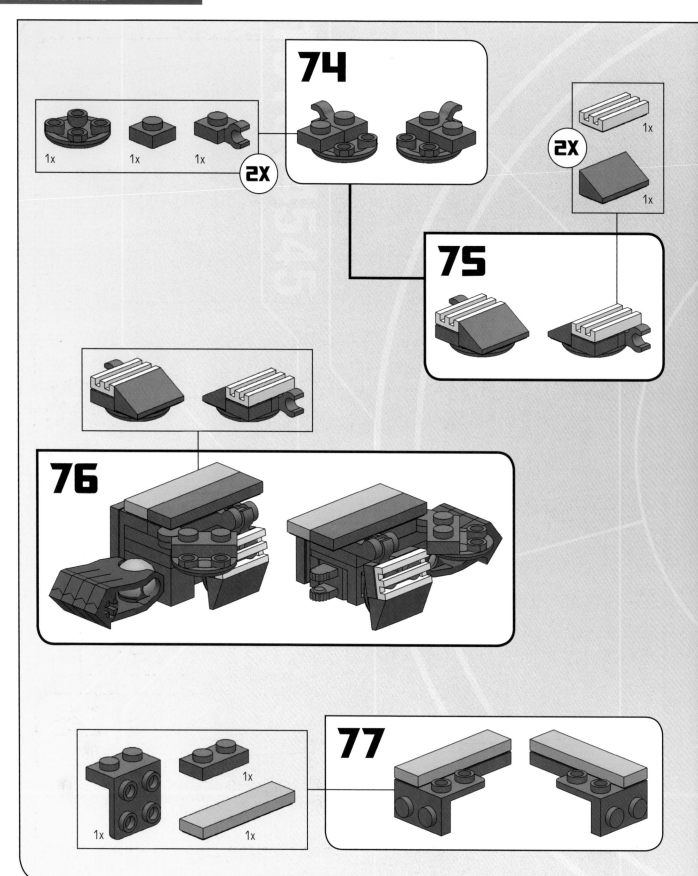

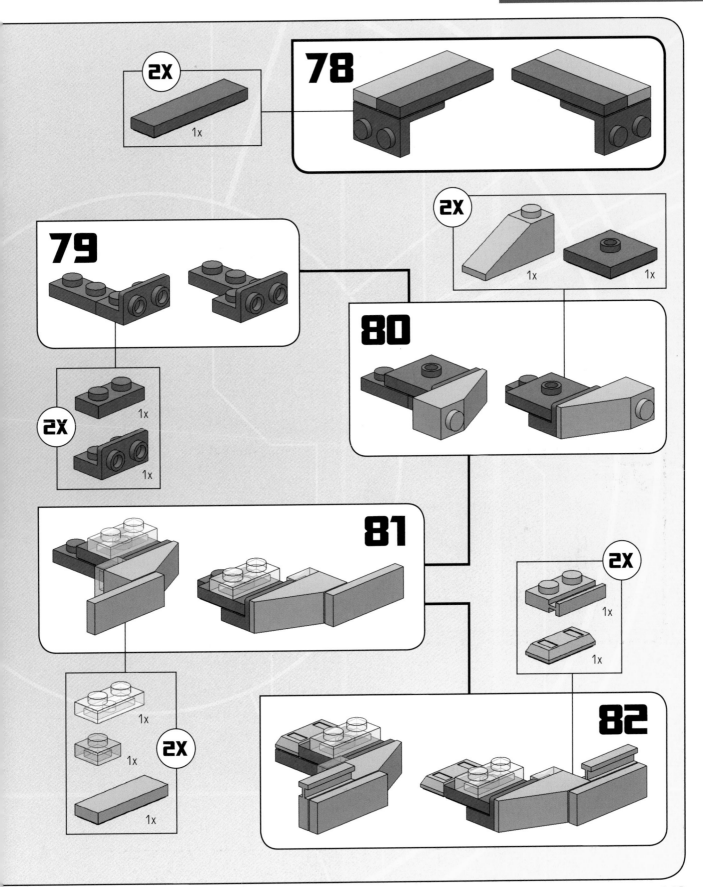

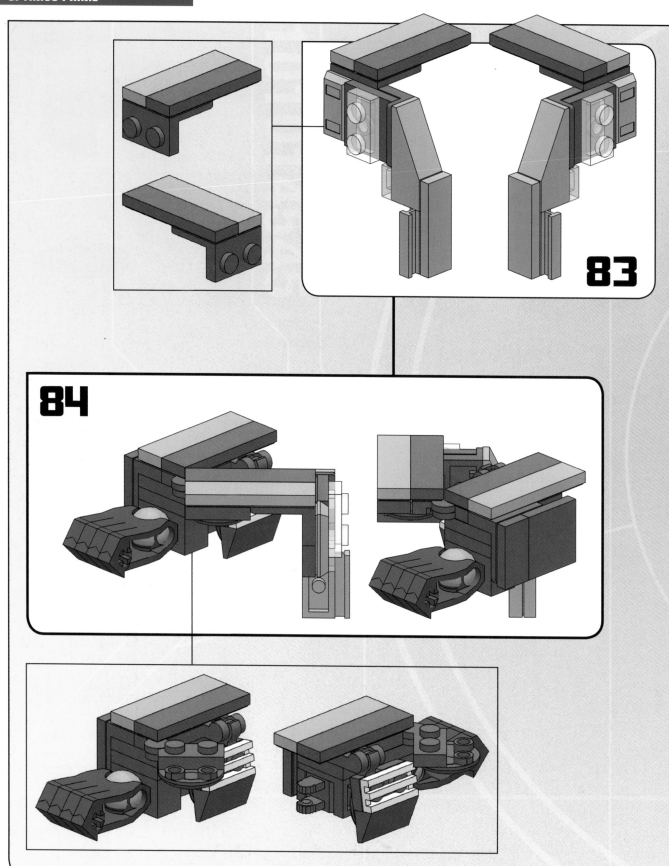

83

84

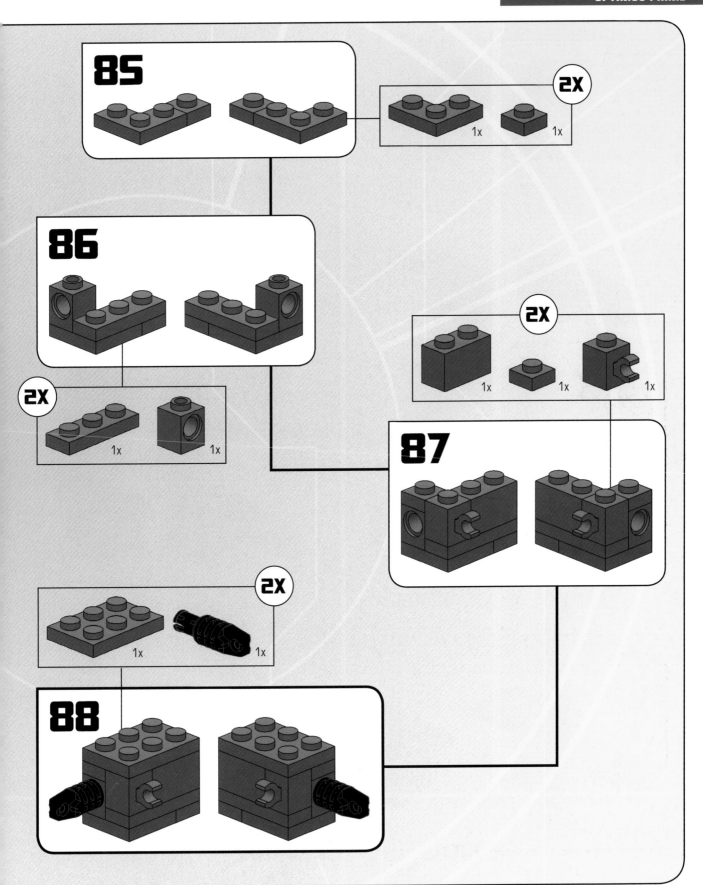

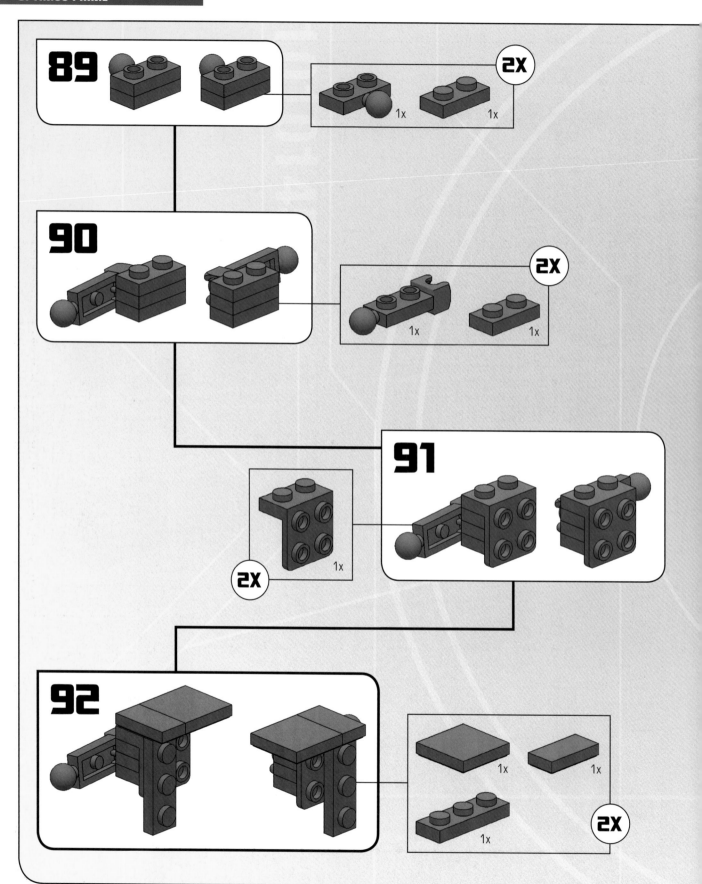

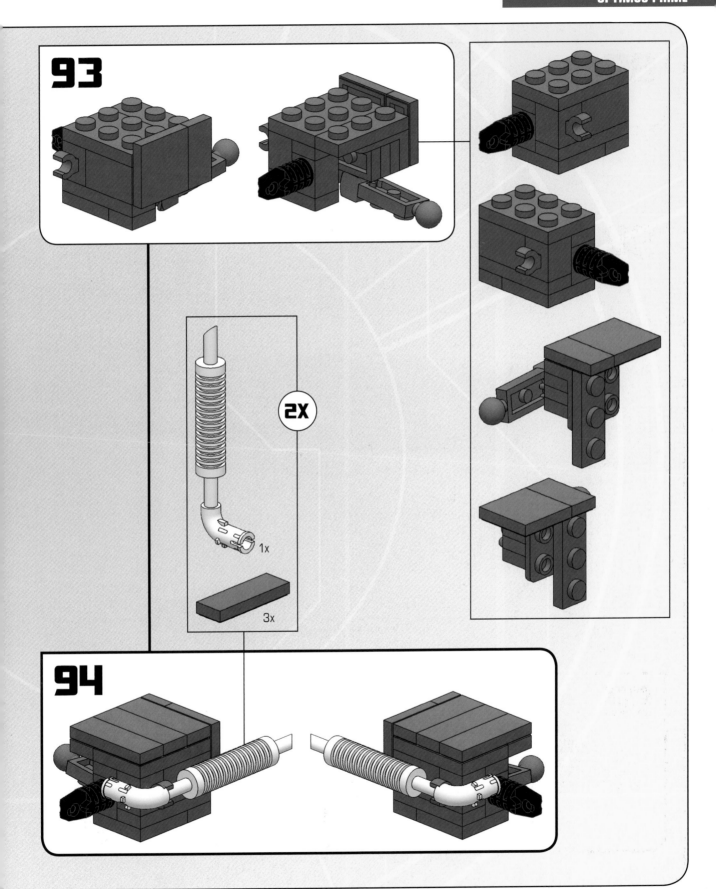

95

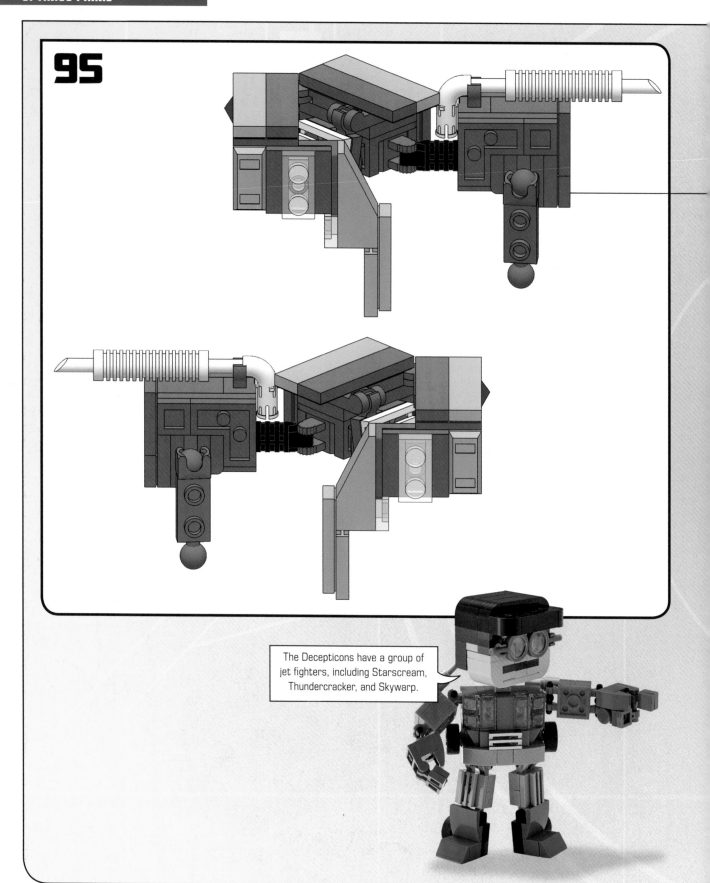

The Decepticons have a group of jet fighters, including Starscream, Thundercracker, and Skywarp.

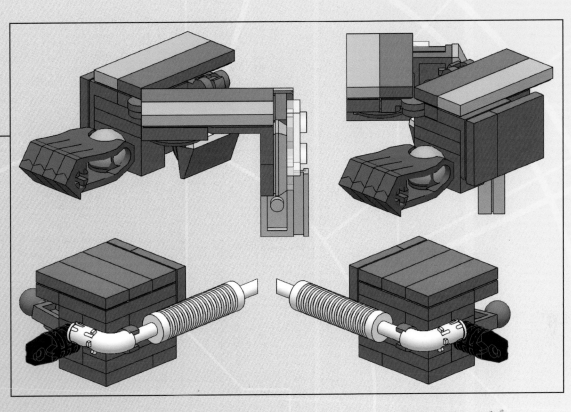

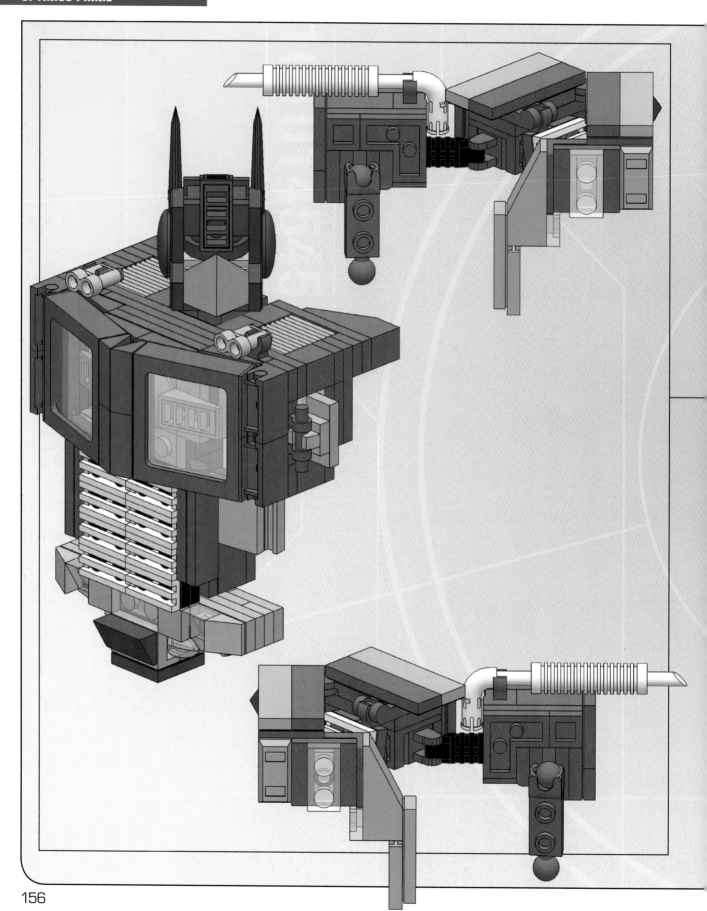

96

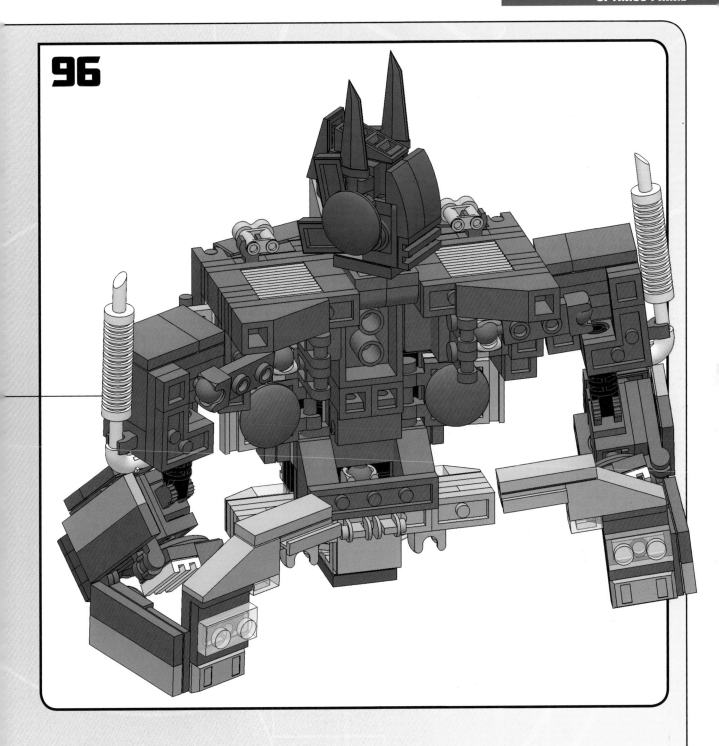

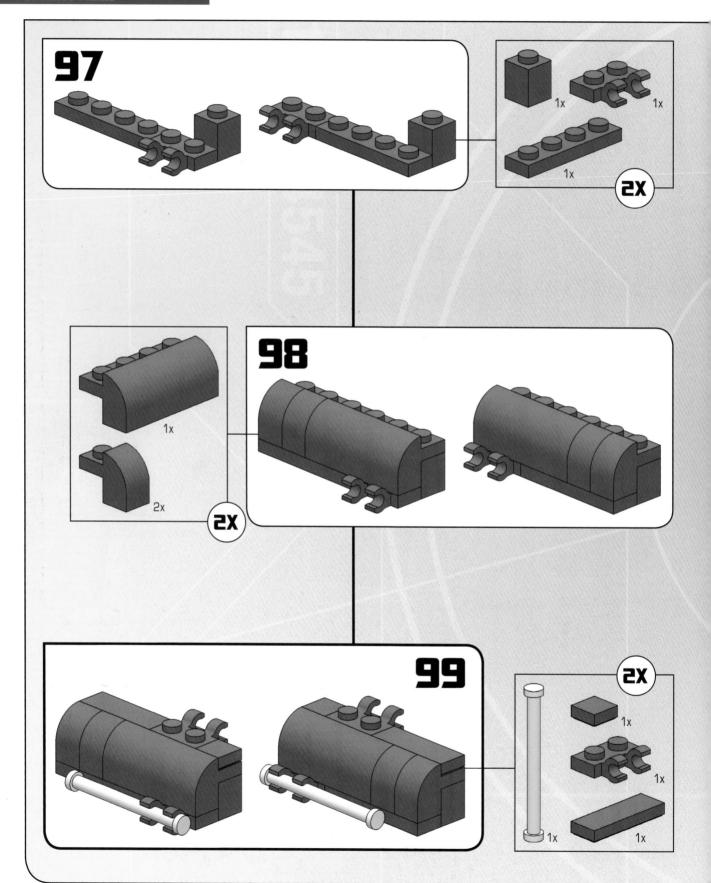

97

1x
1x
1x
2X

98

1x
2x
2X

99

2X
1x
1x
1x
1x

100

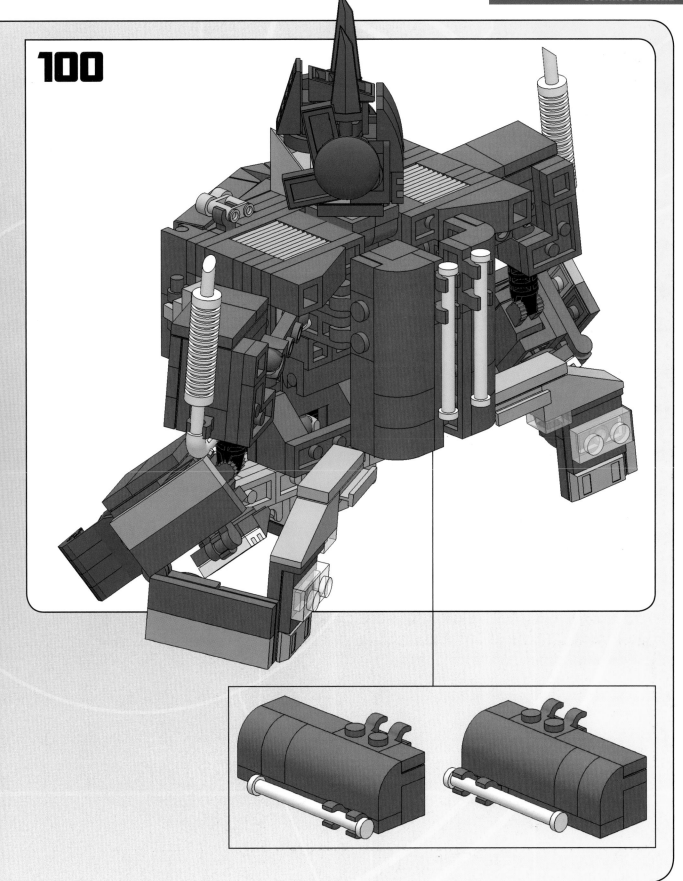

101

4x

102

2x

2x

2x

2x

This brick has studs on one side

103

2x

2x

1x

1x

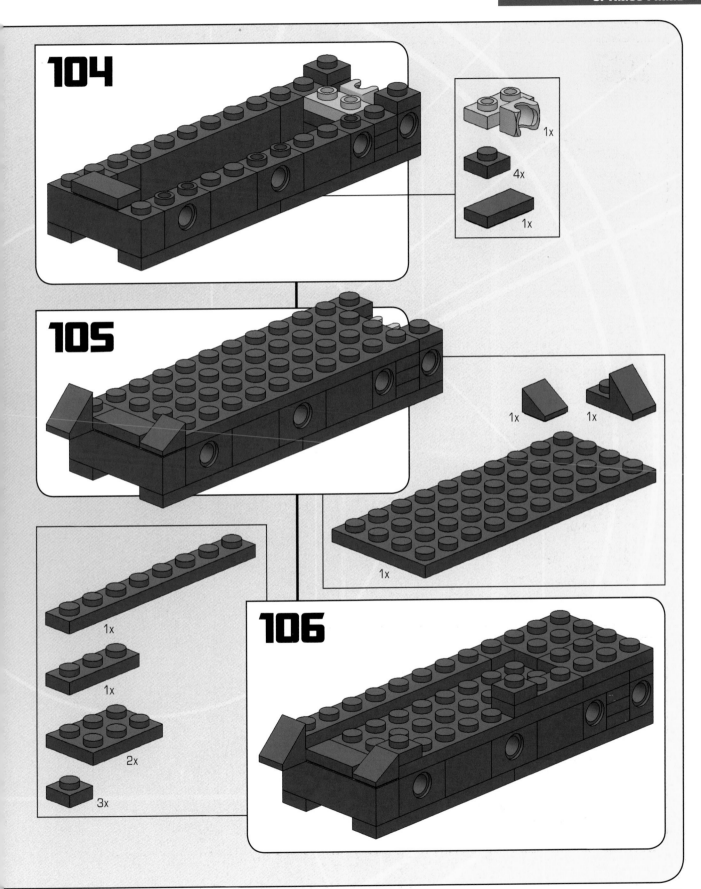

104

1x
4x
1x

105

1x
1x
1x

1x
1x
2x
3x

106

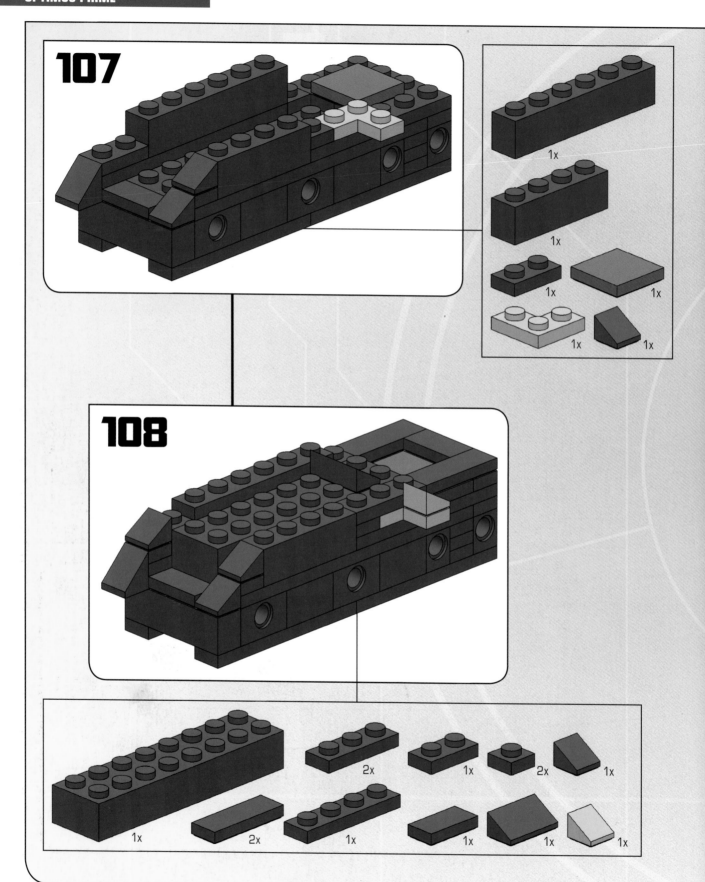

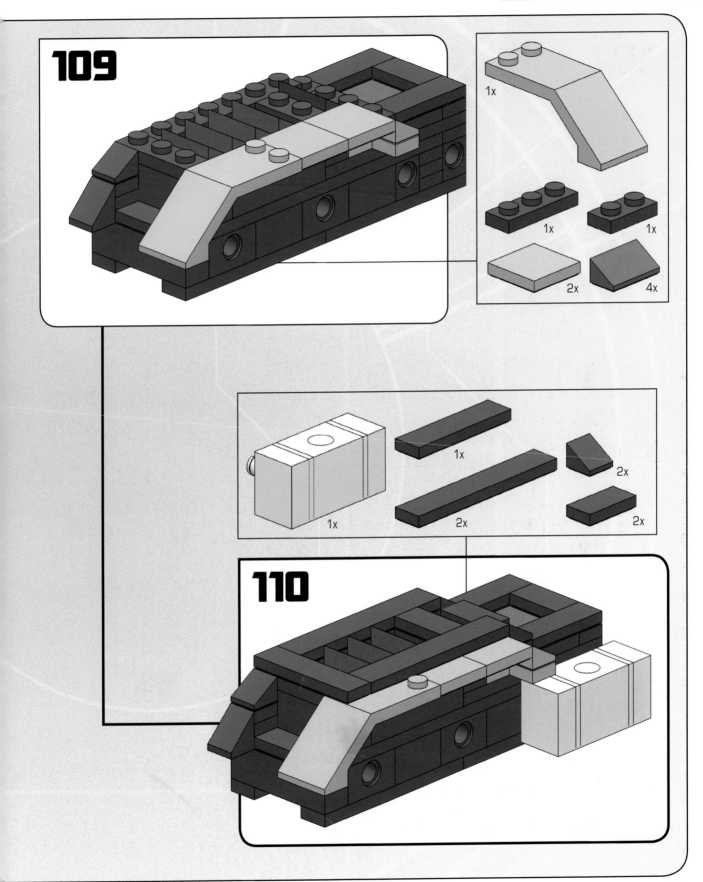

109

1x

1x

1x

2x

4x

1x

1x

2x

2x

2x

110

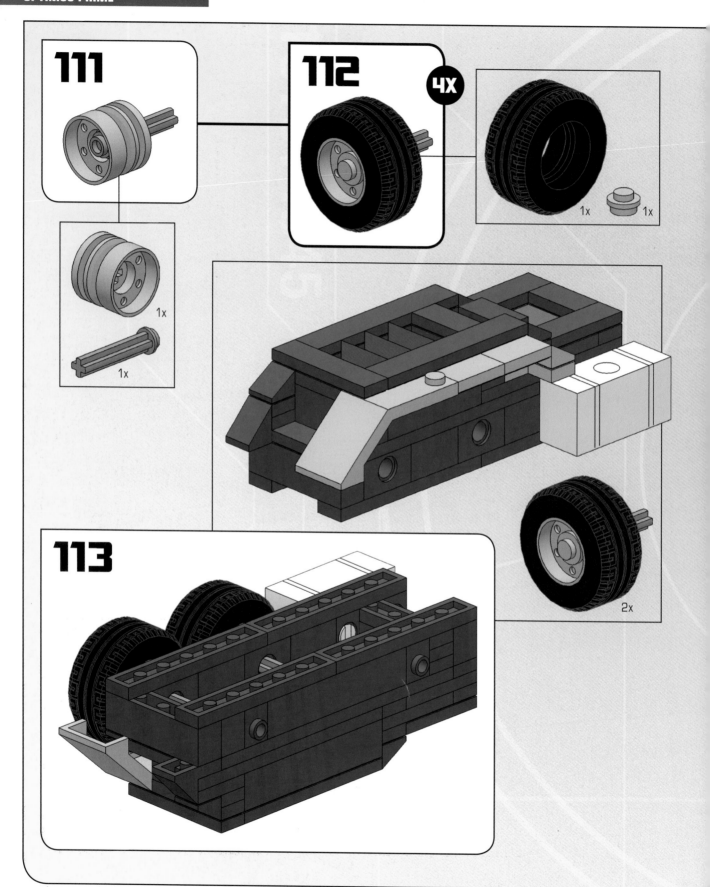

111

112 4X

1x   1x

1x

1x

113

2x

114

2x

115

2x

116

1x

1x

1x

1x

1x

117

1x

2x

118

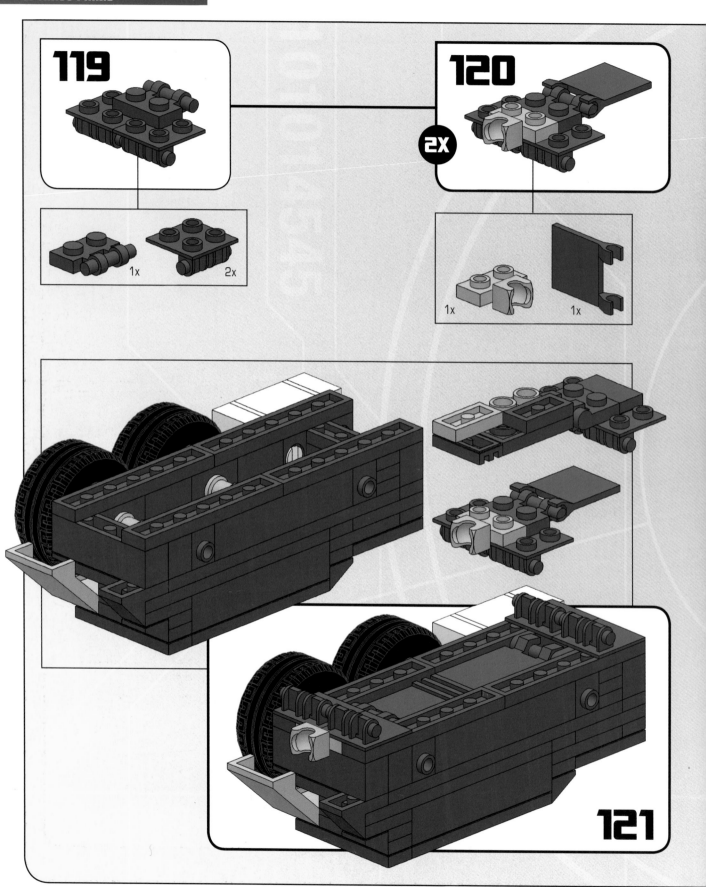

119

1x   2x

120

2X

1x   1x

121

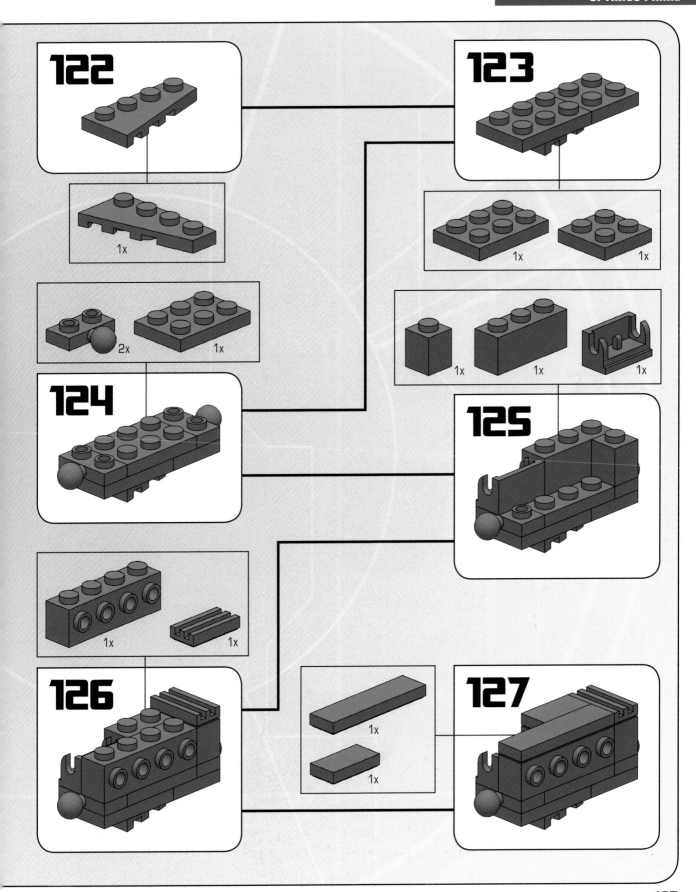

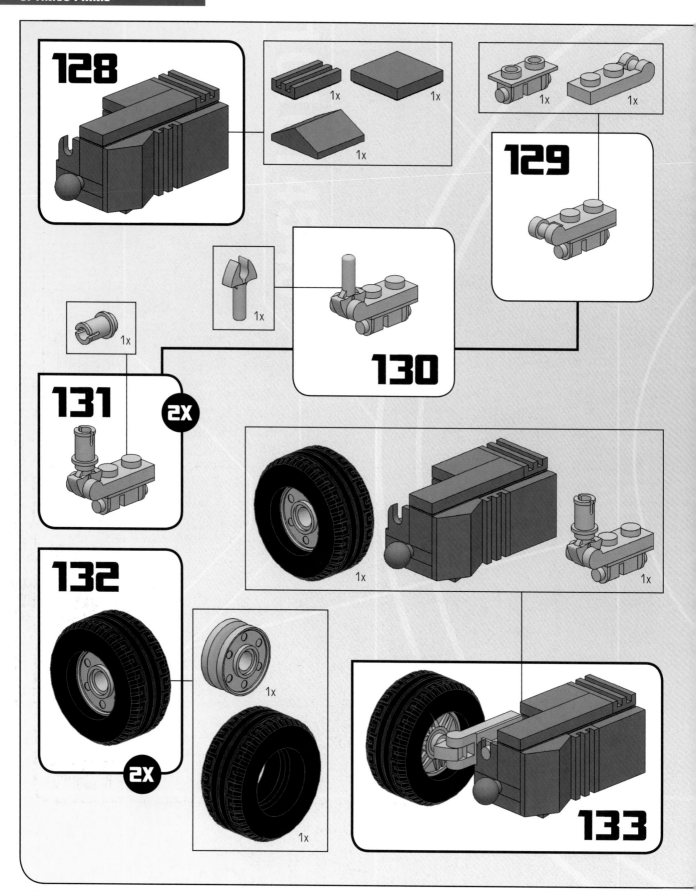

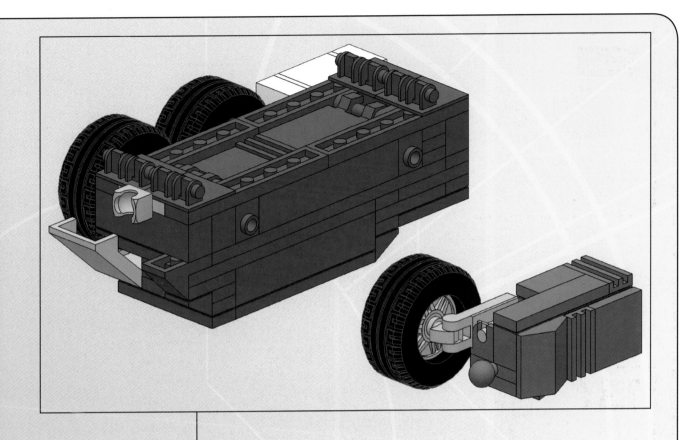

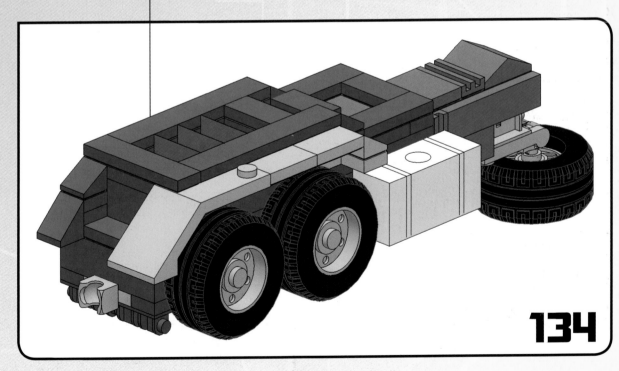

134

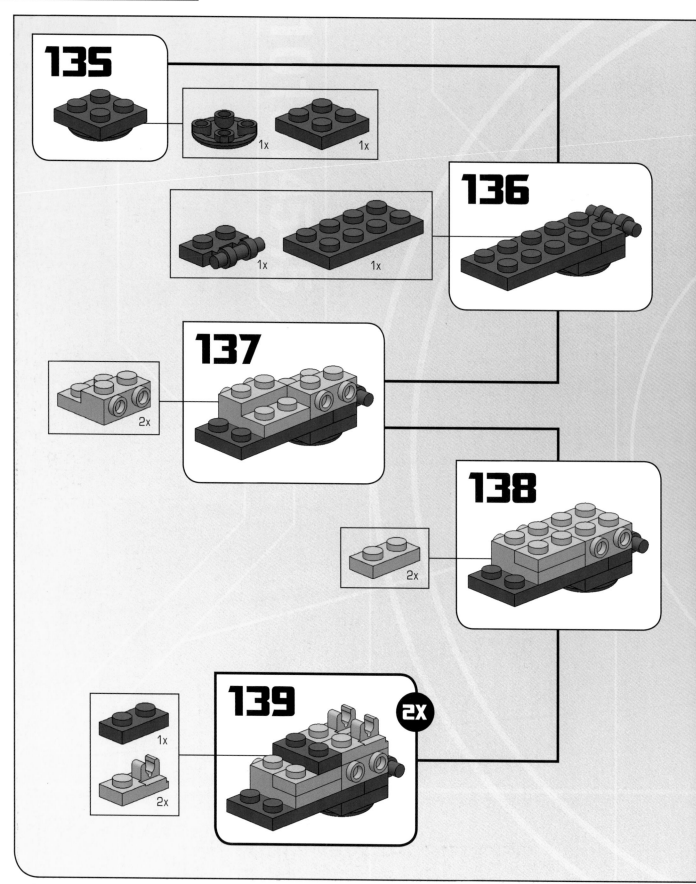

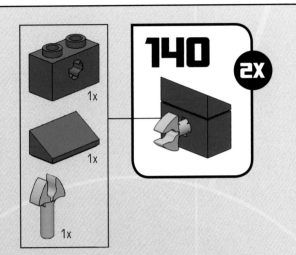

140 2X

141 2X

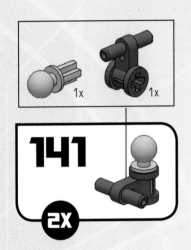

142 2X

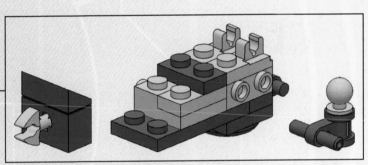

143

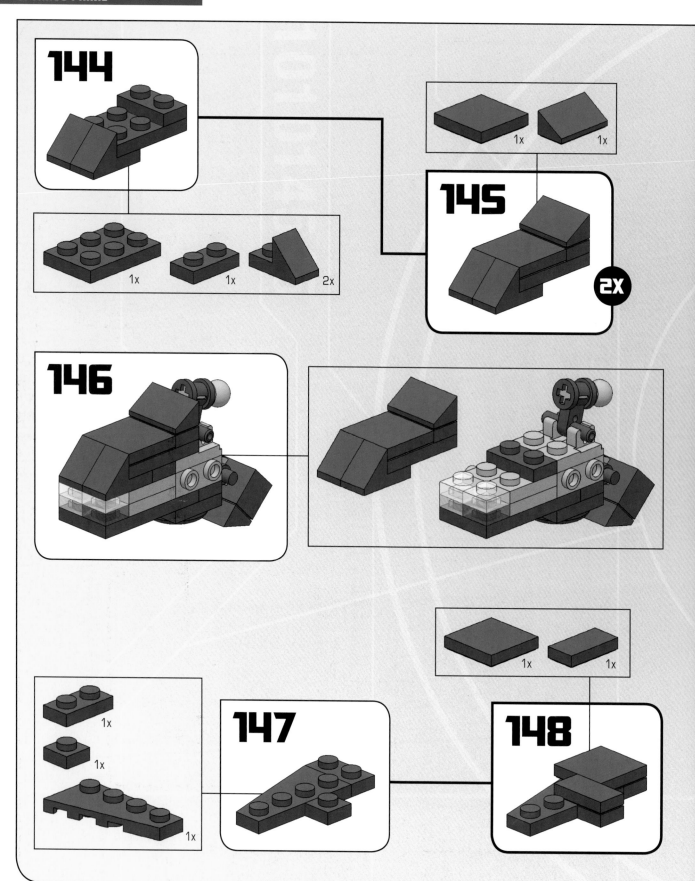

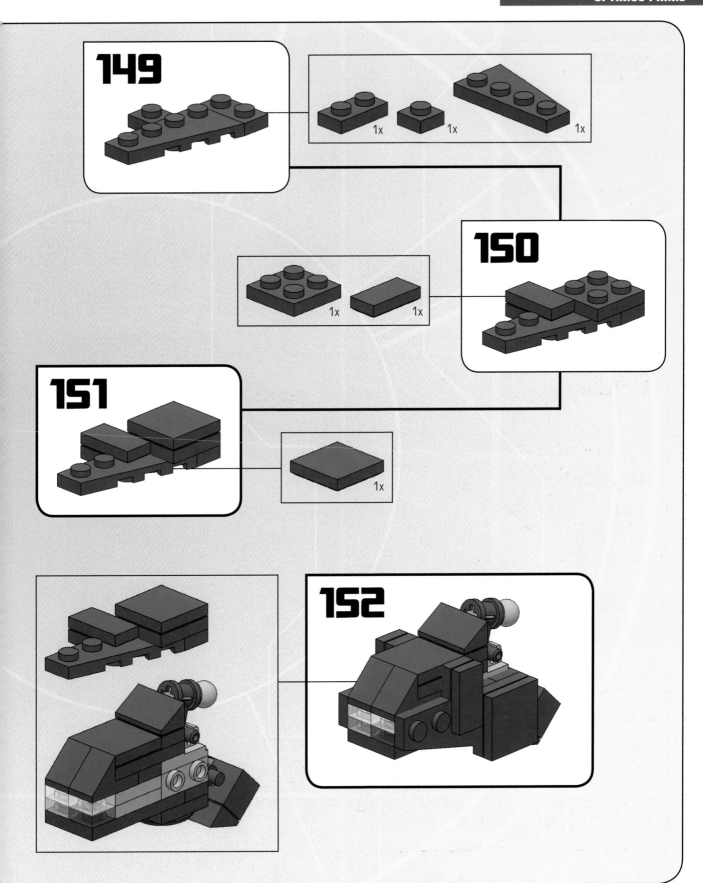

153

154

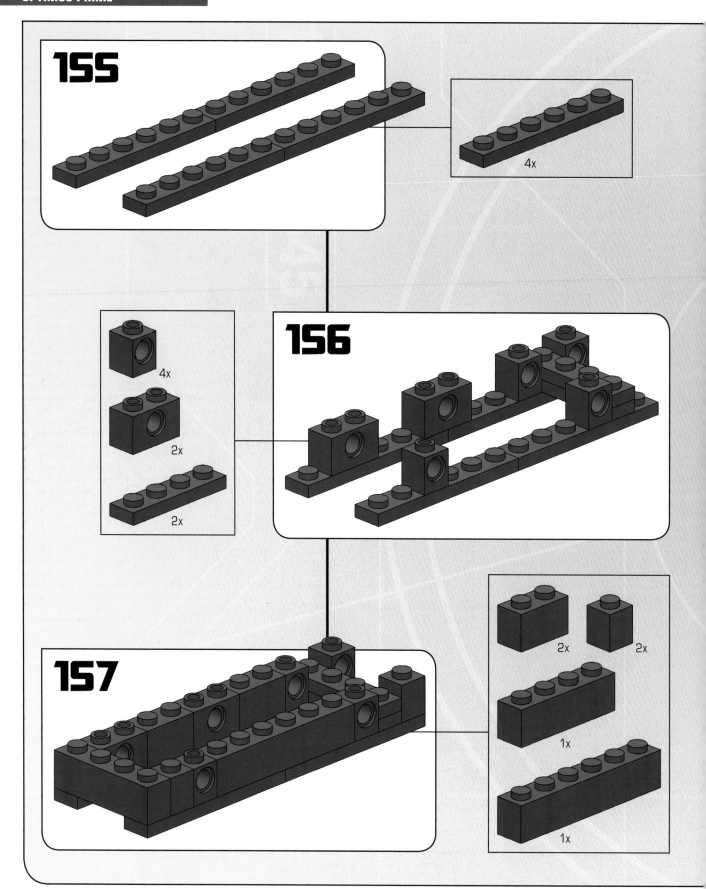

155

4x

156

4x

2x

2x

157

2x   2x

1x

1x

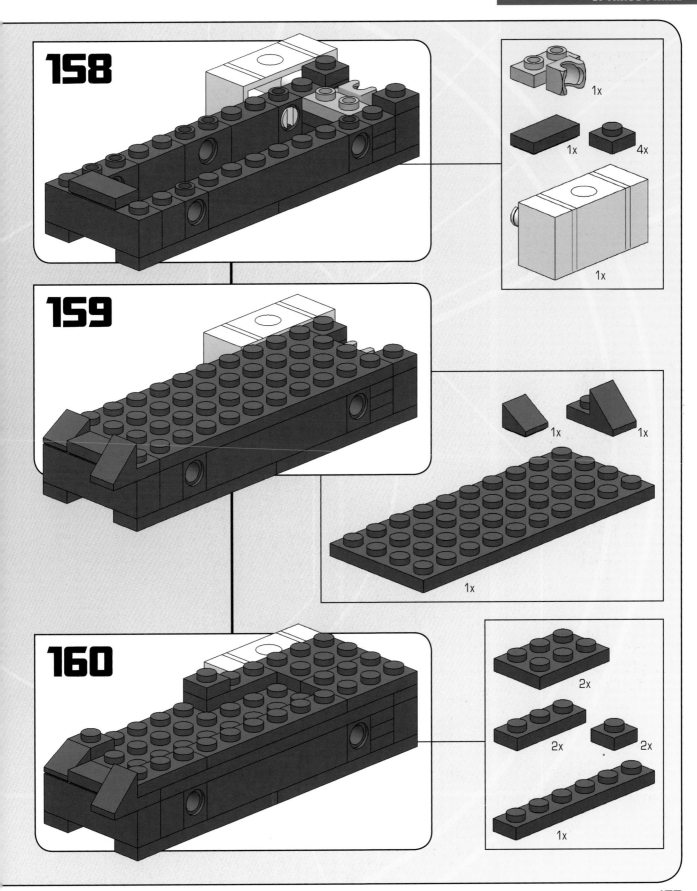

158

1x

1x 4x

1x

159

1x 1x

1x

160

2x

2x 2x

1x

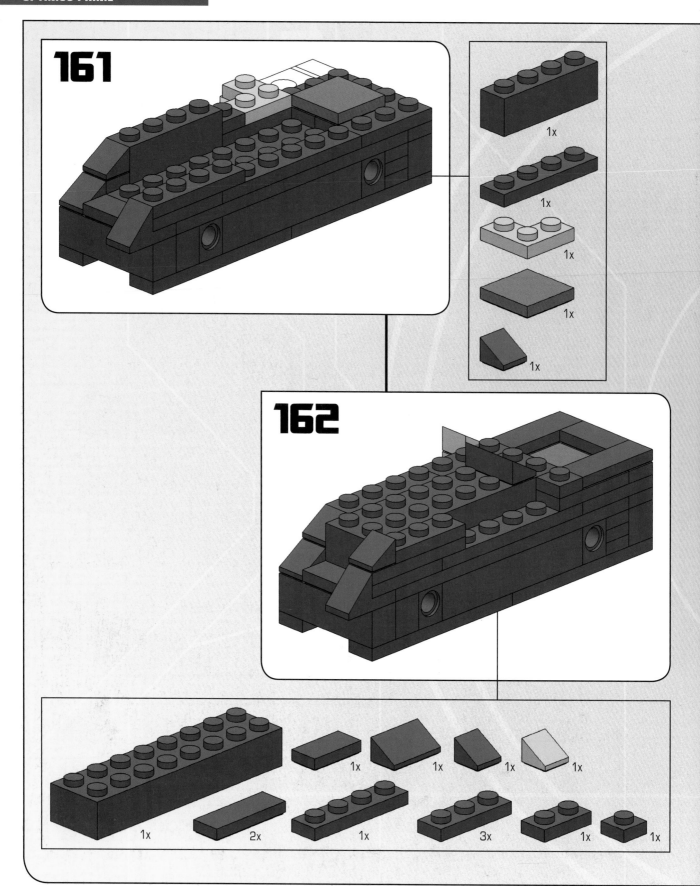

161

1x
1x
1x
1x
1x

162

1x
1x
1x
1x

1x
2x
1x
3x
1x
1x

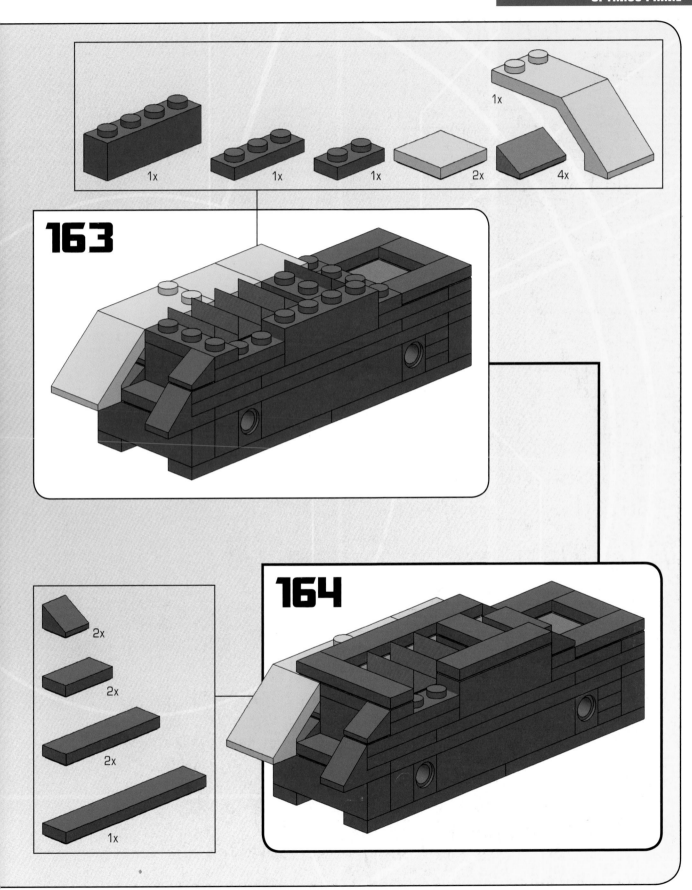

1x
1x
1x
2x
1x
4x

163

164

2x
2x
2x
1x

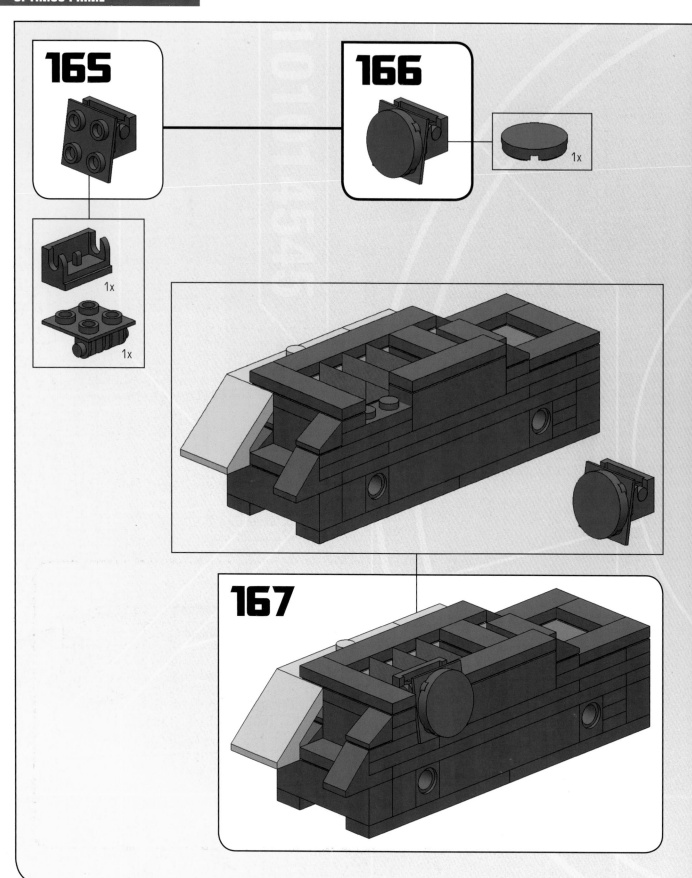

165

166

1x

1x

1x

167

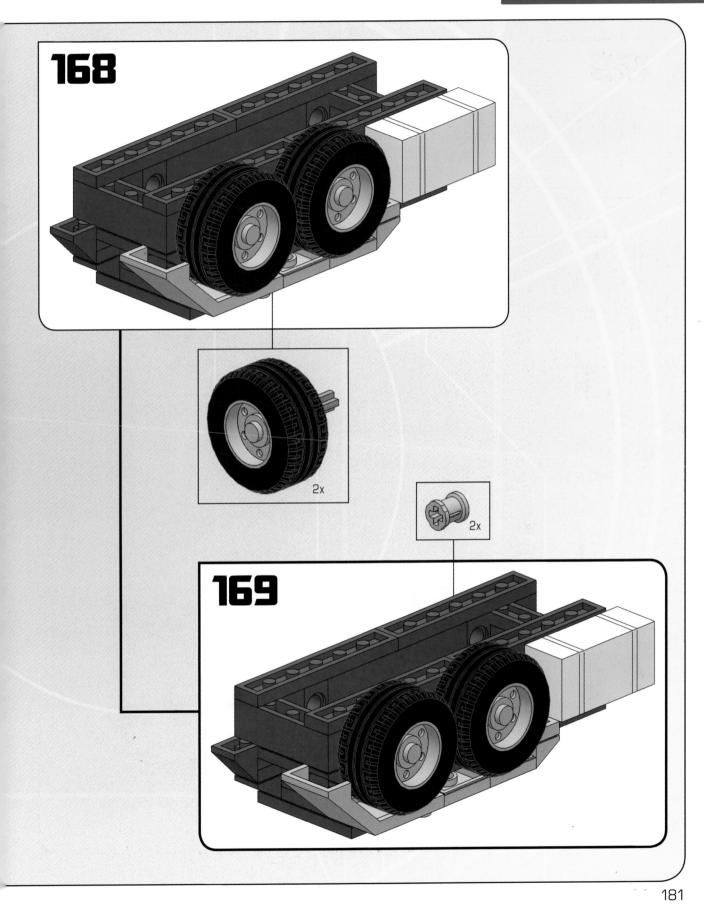

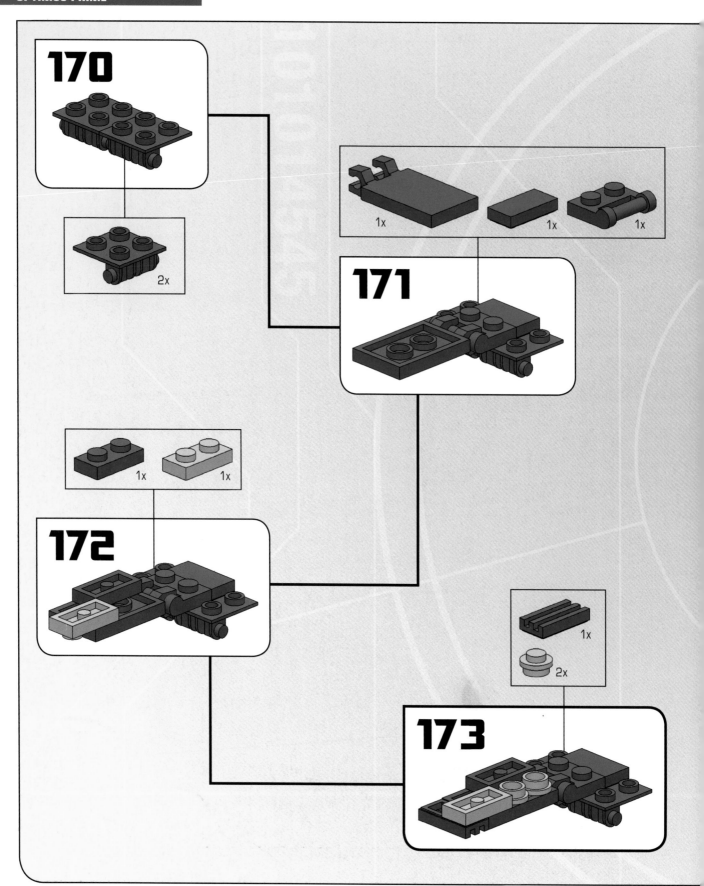

174

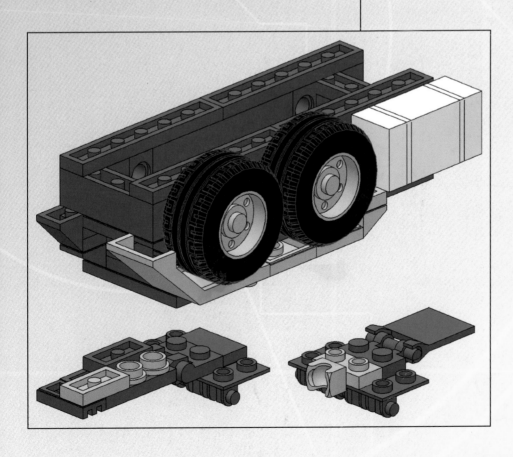

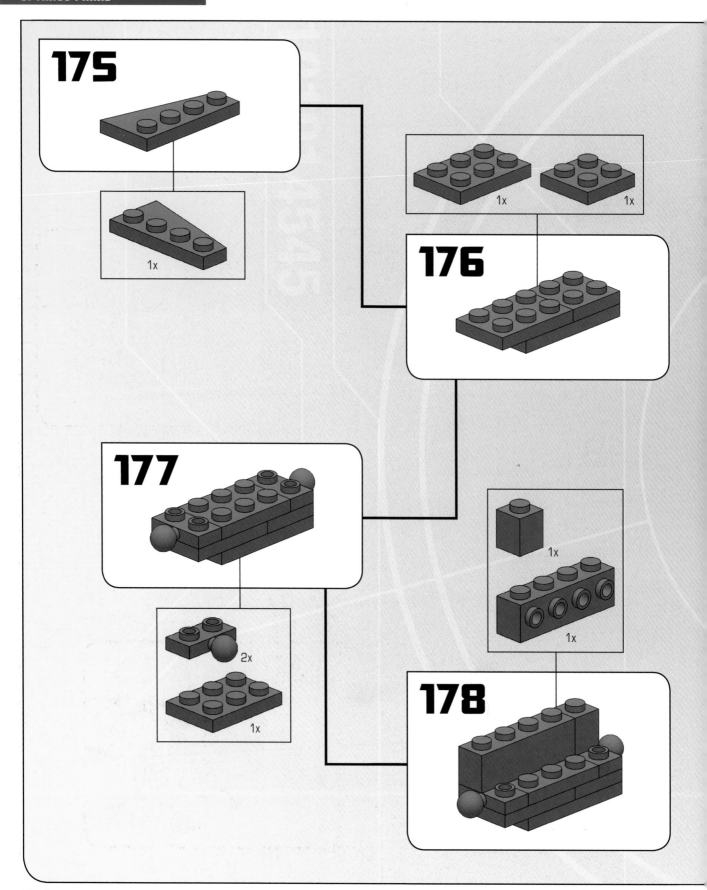

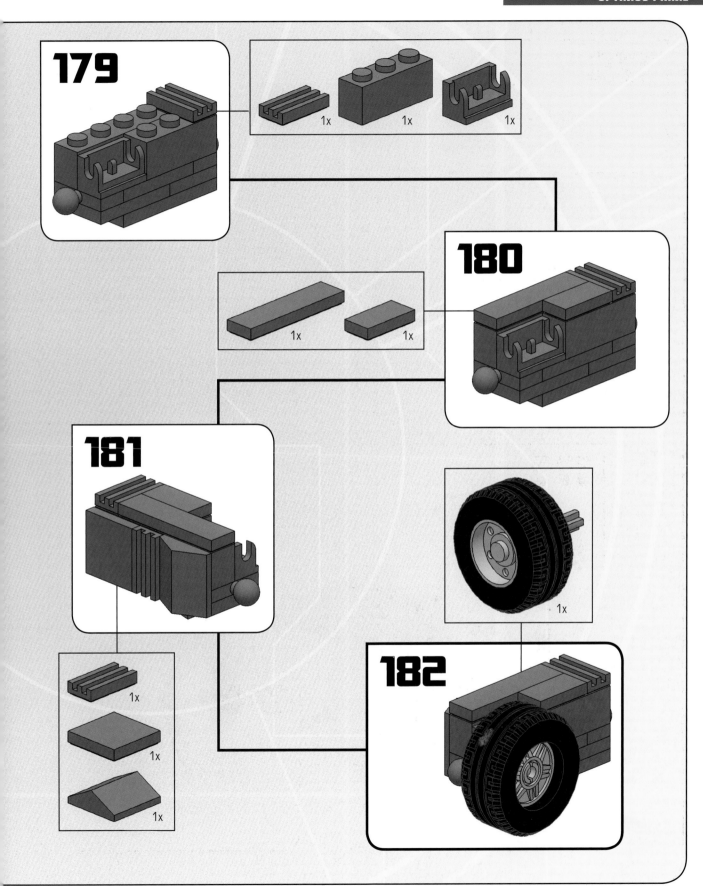

179

1x 1x 1x

180

1x 1x

181

1x
1x
1x

1x

182

183

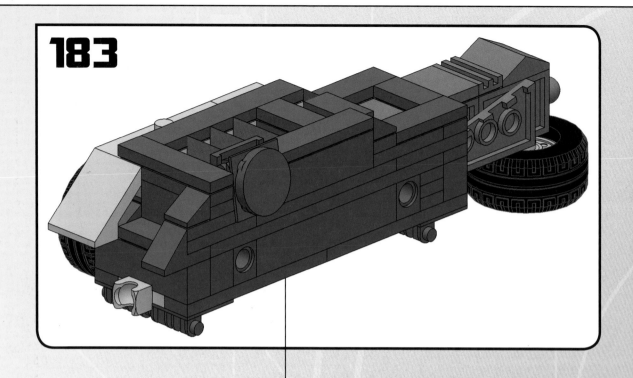

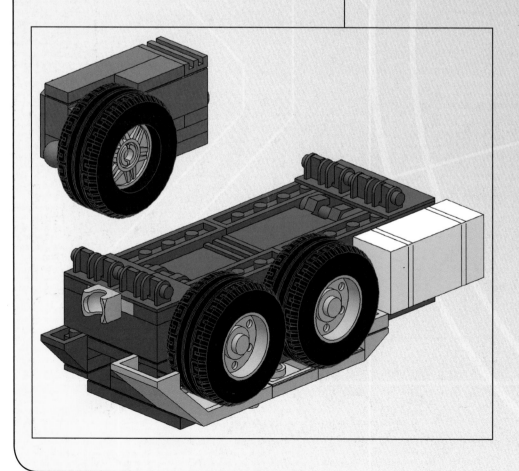

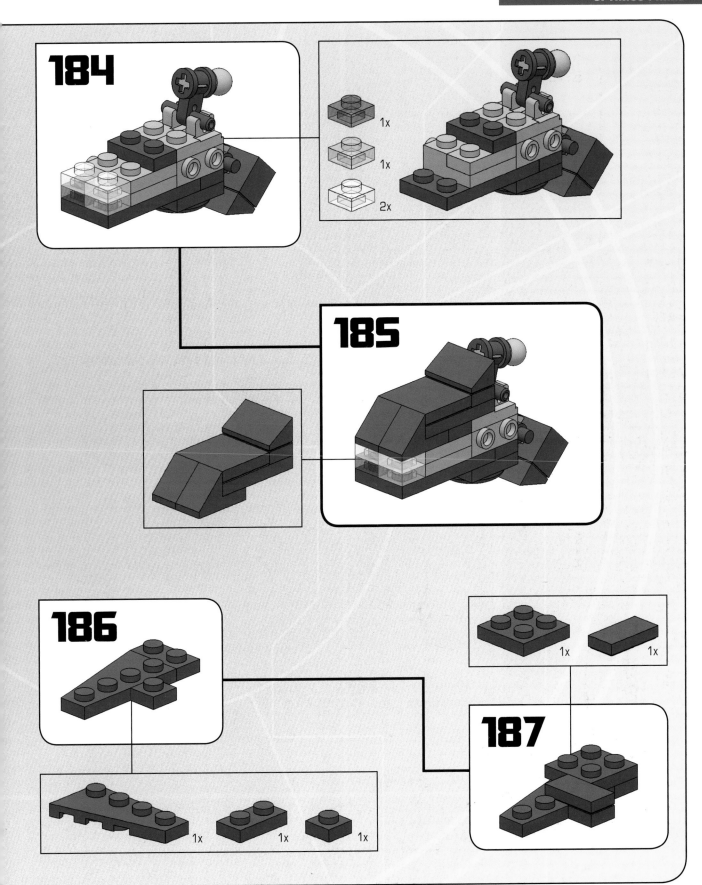

184

1x
1x
2x

185

186

1x
1x

187

1x
1x
1x

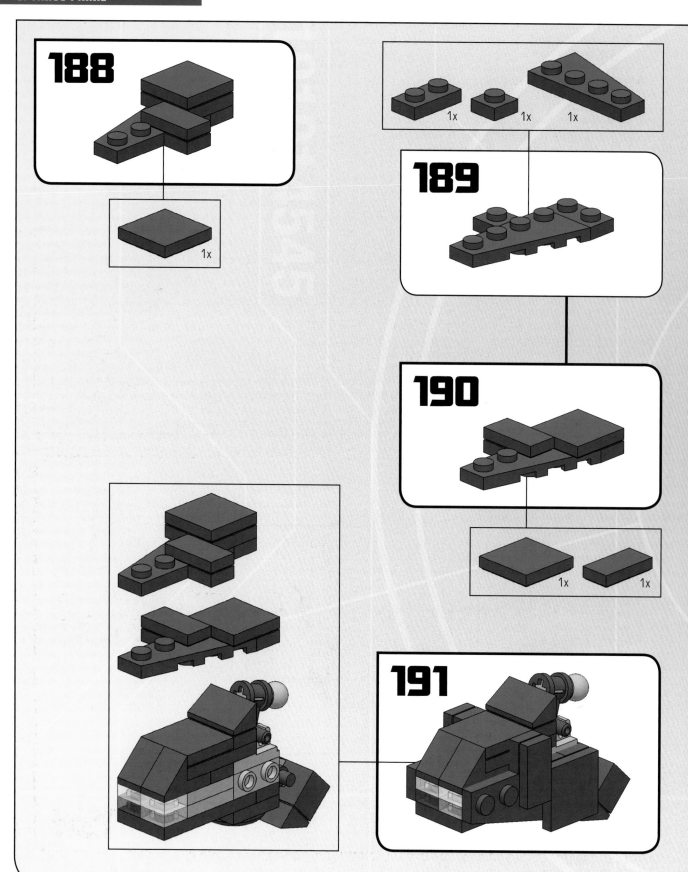

188

1x

189

1x 1x 1x

190

1x 1x

191

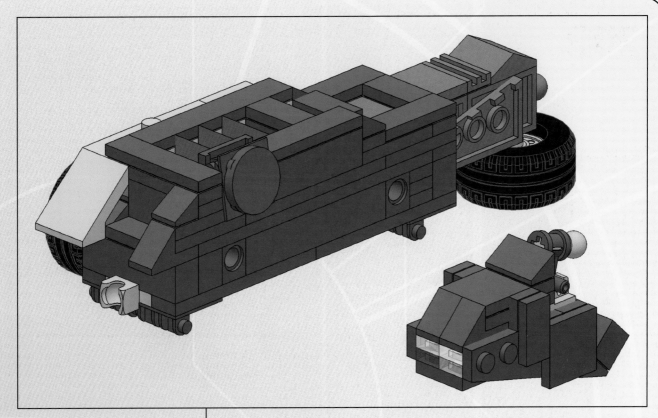

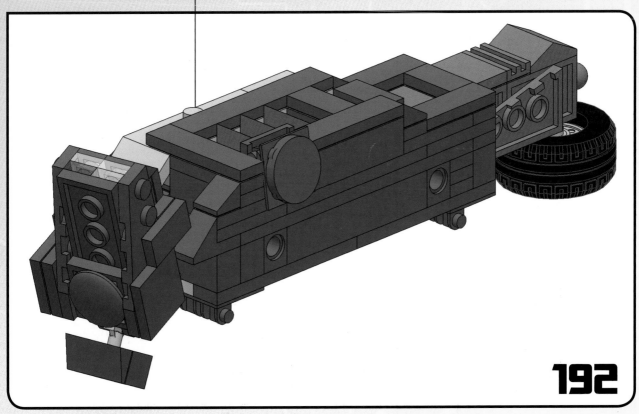

192

193

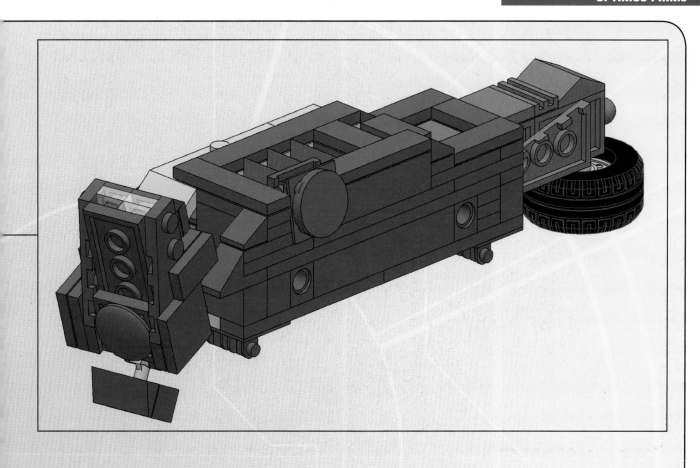

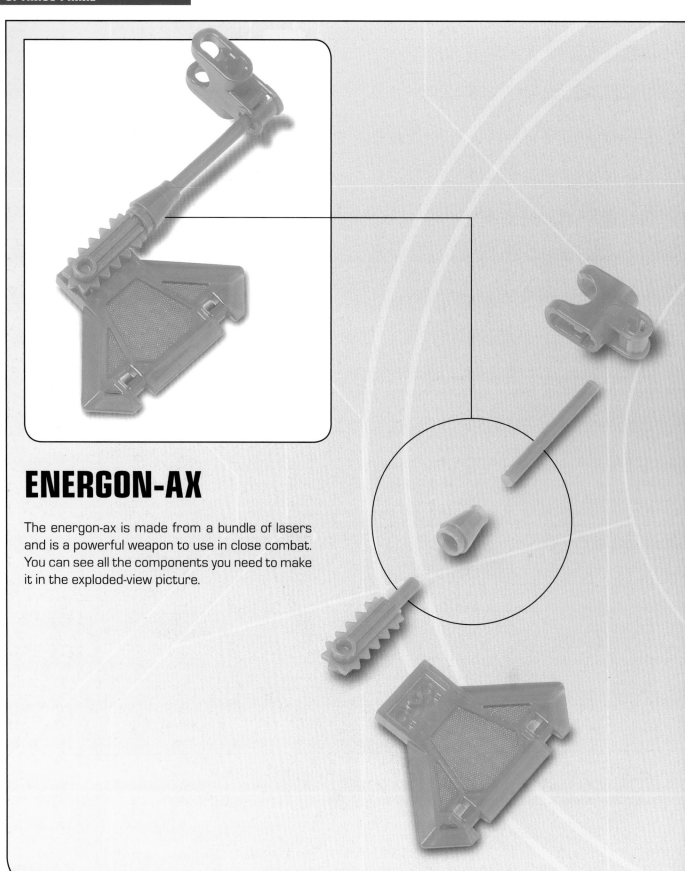

ENERGON-AX

The energon-ax is made from a bundle of lasers and is a powerful weapon to use in close combat. You can see all the components you need to make it in the exploded-view picture.

LASER GUN

So that you can build it, we've here taken apart a mini-version of the otherwise slightly larger main weapon for you. A Technic-Axle connector helps it to fit easily into the hand of the leader of the Autobots.

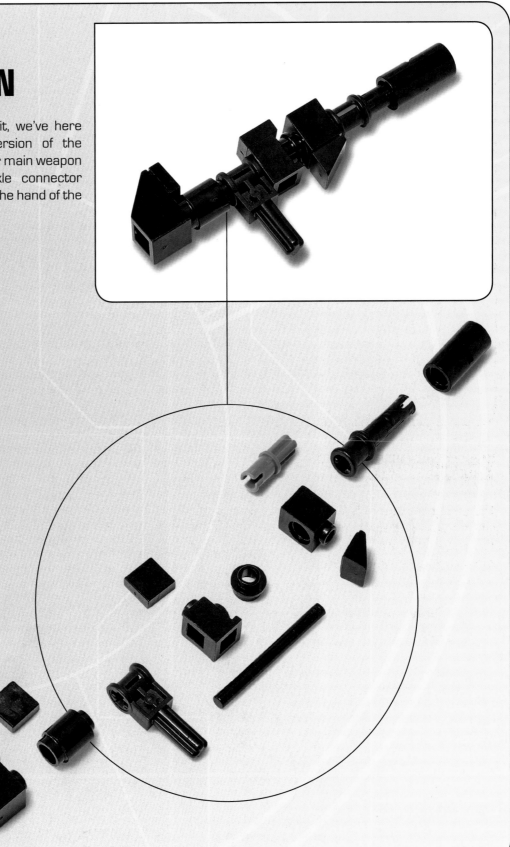

PARTS LIST

Quantity	Color		Element	Element Name	LEGO® Number
4		Light Bluish Gray	55529	Bar 1.5L with Clip	
2		Blue	64727	Bar 0.5L with Blade 3L	4622295
2		Chrome Silver	71184	Bar 4.5L Straight	
2		Light Bluish Gray	99781	Bracket 1 x 2 - 1 x 2 Down	4654582
1		Light Bluish Gray	99780	Bracket 1 x 2 - 1 x 2 Up	6004990
4		Red	99780	Bracket 1 x 2 - 1 x 2 Up	6089698
1		Blue	44728	Bracket 1 x 2 - 2 x 2	4185711, 4505907, 6037412, 6117968
6		Red	44728	Bracket 1 x 2 - 2 x 2	4185525, 4277933, 6048856, 6117974
4		Red	99207	Bracket 1 x 2 - 2 x 2 Up	6001806
4		Blue	3005	Brick 1 x 1	300523
2		Dark Bluish Gray	3005	Brick 1 x 1	4211098
8		Red	3005	Brick 1 x 1	300521
2		Red	60476	Brick 1 x 1 with Clip Horizontal (Thick C-Clip)	4535766
2		Red	4070	Brick 1 x 1 with Headlight	407021
2		Blue	87087	Brick 1 x 1 with Stud on 1 Side	4583862
1		Blue	4733	Brick 1 x 1 with Studs on Four Sides	4296151
4		Blue	3004	Brick 1 x 2	300423, 4613959
2		Red	3004	Brick 1 x 2	300421, 4613961
4		Light Bluish Gray	2877	Brick 1 x 2 with Grille	4211383
2		Trans Clear	3065	Brick 1 x 2 without Centre Stud	306540
2		Dark Bluish Gray	3622	Brick 1 x 3	4211104
5		Blue	3010	Brick 1 x 4	301023
2		Dark Bluish Gray	30414	Brick 1 x 4 with Studs on Side	4210725
3		Blue	3009	Brick 1 x 6	300923
4		Red	6091	Brick 2 x 1 x 1 & 1/3 with Curved Top	609121, 6184782
1		Red	3002	Brick 2 x 3	300221
2		Red	6081	Brick 2 x 4 x 1 & 1/3 with Curved Top	4116617
2		Blue	3007	Brick 2 x 8	300723, 6037384
4		Blue	2654	Dish 2 x 2	4208686, 4278276
6		Red	2654	Dish 2 x 2	4248830, 4278275, 4617080
1		Metallic Gold	4740	Dish 2 x 2 Inverted	6078236
2		Chrome Silver	40620	Exhaust Pipe with Pin	
2		Blue	2335	Flag 2 x 2	4160793, 4523407, 6011816

Quantity		Color	Element	Element Name	LEGO® Number
2		Chrome Silver	45408	Gas Tank 2 x 4 with Technic Pins	
2		Trans Light Blue	3855b	Glass for Window 1 x 4 x 3 without Handle	
2		Light Bluish Gray	96910	Gold Ingot	
1		Blue	3937	Hinge 1 x 2 Base	393723
2		Dark Bluish Gray	3937	Hinge 1 x 2 Base	4211066
5		Red	3937	Hinge 1 x 2 Base	393721
2		Light Bluish Gray	3938	Hinge 1 x 2 Top	4211470
4		Red	3938	Hinge 1 x 2 Top	393821
8		Blue	6134	Hinge 2 x 2 Top	4195007
1		Light Bluish Gray	6134	Hinge 2 x 2 Top	4211881
1		Red	6134	Hinge 2 x 2 Top	613421
2		Black	41532	Hinge Arm Locking with Single Finger and Friction Pin	4159335
2		Red	30365	Hinge Brick 1 x 2 Locking with Dual Finger On End	4173322
2		Red	2429	Hinge Plate 1 x 4 Base	
2		Red	2430	Hinge Plate 1 x 4 Top	
2		Light Bluish Gray	30162	Minifig Binoculars with Round Eyepiece	4550170
21		Blue	3024	Plate 1 x 1	302423
2		Metallic Silver	3024	Plate 1 x 1	4528732
16		Red	3024	Plate 1 x 1	302421
4		Trans Clear	3024	Plate 1 x 1	3000840
2		Trans Red	3024	Plate 1 x 1	3000841
4		Trans Yellow	3024	Plate 1 x 1	3000844
2		Blue	6141	Plate 1 x 1 Round	
8		Light Bluish Gray	6141	Plate 1 x 1 Round	
2		Red	61252	Plate 1 x 1 with Clip Horizontal (Thick C-Clip)	4524644
2		Red	60897	Plate 1 x 1 with Clip Vertical (Thick C-Clip)	
2		Trans Yellow	49668	Plate 1 x 1 with Tooth In-line	4612573
2		Black	3023	Plate 1 x 2	302326
15		Blue	3023	Plate 1 x 2	302323
11		Light Bluish Gray	3023	Plate 1 x 2	3023194, 4211398
13		Red	3023	Plate 1 x 2	302321
2		Trans Clear	3023	Plate 1 x 2	4167842, 622540
1		Trans Light Blue	3023	Plate 1 x 2	6051918

Quantity	Color	Element	Element Name	LEGO® Number
6	Red	60470b	Plate 1 x 2 with 2 Clips Horizontal (Thick C-Clips)	4556153
7	Dark Bluish Gray	14417	Plate 1 x 2 with Ball Joint-8	6039479
4	Light Bluish Gray	32028	Plate 1 x 2 with Door Rail	4211568
4	Blue	2540	Plate 1 x 2 with Handle	254023, 4140586
2	Red	2540	Plate 1 x 2 with Handle	254021, 4140585
2	Light Bluish Gray	60478	Plate 1 x 2 with Handle on End	4515369
6	Red	60478	Plate 1 x 2 with Handle on End	4515365
2	Blue	48336	Plate 1 x 2 with Handle Type 2	4247103, 4514398
2	Red	48336	Plate 1 x 2 with Handle Type 2	4226876
2	Dark Bluish Gray	11458	Plate 1 x 2 with Offset Peghole	6019987
4	Light Bluish Gray	92280	Plate 1 x 2 with Single Clip on Top	4598526
2	Dark Bluish Gray	14419	Plate 1 x 2 with Socket Joint-8 with Friction and Ball Joint-8	6039482
9	Light Bluish Gray	14704	Plate 1 x 2 with Socket Joint-8 with Friction Centre	6043656
1	Blue	3794	Plate 1 x 2 without Groove with 1 Centre Stud	379423
4	Light Bluish Gray	3794	Plate 1 x 2 without Groove with 1 Centre Stud	4211451
10	Blue	3623	Plate 1 x 3	362323
2	Light Bluish Gray	3623	Plate 1 x 3	3623194, 4211429
10	Red	3623	Plate 1 x 3	362321
7	Blue	3710	Plate 1 x 4	371023
1	Light Bluish Gray	3710	Plate 1 x 4	4211445
5	Red	3710	Plate 1 x 4	371021
1	Red	92593	Plate 1 x 4 with Two Studs	4631877
9	Blue	3666	Plate 1 x 6	366623
1	Red	3666	Plate 1 x 6	366621
1	Blue	3460	Plate 1 x 8	346023
1	Red	4477	Plate 1 x 10	447721
4	Blue	3022	Plate 2 x 2	302223, 4613973
2	Dark Bluish Gray	3022	Plate 2 x 2	4211094
1	Light Bluish Gray	3022	Plate 2 x 2	4211397
2	Light Bluish Gray	2420	Plate 2 x 2 Corner	4211353
4	Metallic Silver	2420	Plate 2 x 2 Corner	4528731
4	Red	2420	Plate 2 x 2 Corner	242021
1	Light Bluish Gray	87580	Plate 2 x 2 with Groove with 1 Center Stud	4565393, 6126082

Quantity		Color	Element	Element Name	LEGO® Number
2		Red	87580	Plate 2 x 2 with Groove with 1 Center Stud	4581308, 6126048
2		Black	99206	Plate 2 x 2 x 0.667 with Two Studs On Side and Two Raised	6052126
4		Light Bluish Gray	99206	Plate 2 x 2 x 0.667 with Two Studs On Side and Two Raised	4654577
6		Blue	3021	Plate 2 x 3	302123
4		Dark Bluish Gray	3021	Plate 2 x 3	4211043
4		Red	3021	Plate 2 x 3	302121
2		Black	3020	Plate 2 x 4	302026
2		Blue	3020	Plate 2 x 4	302023
1		Red	3020	Plate 2 x 4	302021
1		Blue	3176	Plate 3 x 2 with Hole	317623
2		Blue	3030	Plate 4 x 10	303023
2		Blue	61409	Slope Brick 18 2 x 1 x 2/3 Grille	4597338
2		Light Bluish Gray	61409	Slope Brick 18 2 x 1 x 2/3 Grille	6092111
4		Red	61409	Slope Brick 18 2 x 1 x 2/3 Grille	4535102, 4540382
10		Blue	54200	Slope Brick 31 1 x 1 x 2/3	4296154, 4504380
4		Metallic Silver	54200	Slope Brick 31 1 x 1 x 2/3	4528609, 6092109
2		Trans Yellow	54200	Slope Brick 31 1 x 1 x 2/3	4244367, 4260942
7		Blue	85984	Slope Brick 31 1 x 2 x 2/3	4651236
8		Dark Bluish Gray	85984	Slope Brick 31 1 x 2 x 2/3	4567887
6		Red	85984	Slope Brick 31 1 x 2 x 2/3	4651524
2		Dark Bluish Gray	3300	Slope Brick 33 2 x 2 Double	4212312, 4523365
2		Light Bluish Gray	4286	Slope Brick 33 3 x 1	4211488
2		Red	4287	Slope Brick 33 3 x 1 Inverted	428721
2		Light Bluish Gray	3298	Slope Brick 33 3 x 2	4211421
1		Light Bluish Gray	3049c	Slope Brick 45 1 x 2 Double / Inverted without Centre Stud	4653091
2		Red	3665	Slope Brick 45 2 x 1 Inverted with Inner Stopper Ring	366521
2		Blue	11477	Slope Brick Curved 2 x 1	6055065
6		Blue	92946	Slope Plate 45 2 x 1	4620297, 6069163
4		Dark Tan	6587	Technic Axle 3 with Stud	4566927, 6031821
2		Blue	43093	Technic Axle Pin with Friction	4206482, 4309323
2		Light Bluish Gray	2736	Technic Axle Towball	4211375
2		Light Bluish Gray	32474	Technic Ball Joint with Axlehole Blind	4290716, 4585707, 6070731

Quantity	Color	Element	Element Name	LEGO® Number
8	Blue	6541	Technic Brick 1 x 1 with Hole	4119014
4	Red	6541	Technic Brick 1 x 1 with Hole	654121
2	Blue	32064b	Technic Brick 1 x 2 with Axlehole Type 2	4233490
4	Blue	3700	Technic Brick 1 x 2 with Hole	370023
2	Red	3700	Technic Brick 1 x 2 with Hole	370021
4	Light Bluish Gray	3713	Technic Bush with Two Flanges	4211622
2	Light Bluish Gray	4274	Technic Pin 1/2	4211483, 4274194
2	Black	2780	Technic Pin with Friction and Slots	278026, 4121715
2	Blue	99021	Technic Pneumatic Hose Connector with Bush	4648927
1	Trans Light Blue	98138	Tile 1 x 1 Round with Groove	6022171
2	Light Bluish Gray	2555	Tile 1 x 1 with Clip	2555194, 4211369, 6030711
2	Blue	93794	Tile 1 x 1 with Clip with Centre Notch	
2	Light Bluish Gray	3070b	Tile 1 x 1 with Groove	4211415
4	Red	3070b	Tile 1 x 1 with Groove	307021
3	Blue	2412b	Tile 1 x 2 Grille with Groove	241223
10	Chrome Silver	2412b	Tile 1 x 2 Grille with Groove	4116794
4	Dark Bluish Gray	2412b	Tile 1 x 2 Grille with Groove	4210631
18	Blue	3069b	Tile 1 x 2 with Groove	306923
2	Dark Bluish Gray	3069b	Tile 1 x 2 with Groove	4211052
9	Red	3069b	Tile 1 x 2 with Groove	306921
1	Trans Yellow	3069b	Tile 1 x 2 with Groove	3007044, 306944, 4194535
4	Blue	63864	Tile 1 x 3 with Groove	4587840
2	Light Bluish Gray	63864	Tile 1 x 3 with Groove	4558169
10	Red	63864	Tile 1 x 3 with Groove	4533742
3	Blue	2431	Tile 1 x 4 with Groove	243123
2	Dark Bluish Gray	2431	Tile 1 x 4 with Groove	4211053
4	Light Bluish Gray	2431	Tile 1 x 4 with Groove	2431194, 4211356
4	Red	2431	Tile 1 x 4 with Groove	243121
3	Blue	6636	Tile 1 x 6	4118785
1	Blue	4150	Tile 2 x 2 Round with Cross Underside Stud	415023, 4239001
7	Blue	3068b	Tile 2 x 2 with Groove	306823
4	Dark Bluish Gray	3068b	Tile 2 x 2 with Groove	4211055
6	Metallic Silver	3068b	Tile 2 x 2 with Groove	4528741
4	Red	3068b	Tile 2 x 2 with Groove	306821

Quantity		Color	Element	Element Name	LEGO® Number
2		Blue	30350	Tile 2 x 3 with Horizontal Clips	
2		Red	6556	Train Window 1 x 4 x 3 with Shutter Holes	4513548, 4598324
1		Blue	3680	Turntable 2 x 2 Plate Base	368023
1		Light Bluish Gray	3679	Turntable 2 x 2 Plate Top	4211439, 4495467, 4540203
6		Black	58090	Tyre 14/ 54 x 15 VR	4500518, 4550937
2		Light Bluish Gray	56902	Wheel Rim 8 x 18 with Deep Centre Groove and Peghole	4499259
4		Light Bluish Gray	55982	Wheel Rim 14 x 18 with Axlehole	4490127
2		Metallic Silver	6070	Windscreen 5 x 2 x 1.667	4550286
2		Blue	41770	Wing 2 x 4 Left	4161330
1		Dark Bluish Gray	41770	Wing 2 x 4 Left	4210788
1		Light Bluish Gray	41770	Wing 2 x 4 Left	4211735
2		Blue	41769	Wing 2 x 4 Right	4160867
1		Dark Bluish Gray	41769	Wing 2 x 4 Right	4210782
1		Light Bluish Gray	41769	Wing 2 x 4 Right	4211732
2		Blue	93575	Hero Factory Fist with Axle Hole	4610919

4x

2x

2x

1x

4x

4x

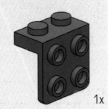
1x

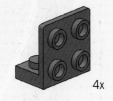
6x

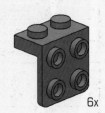
4x

4x

2x

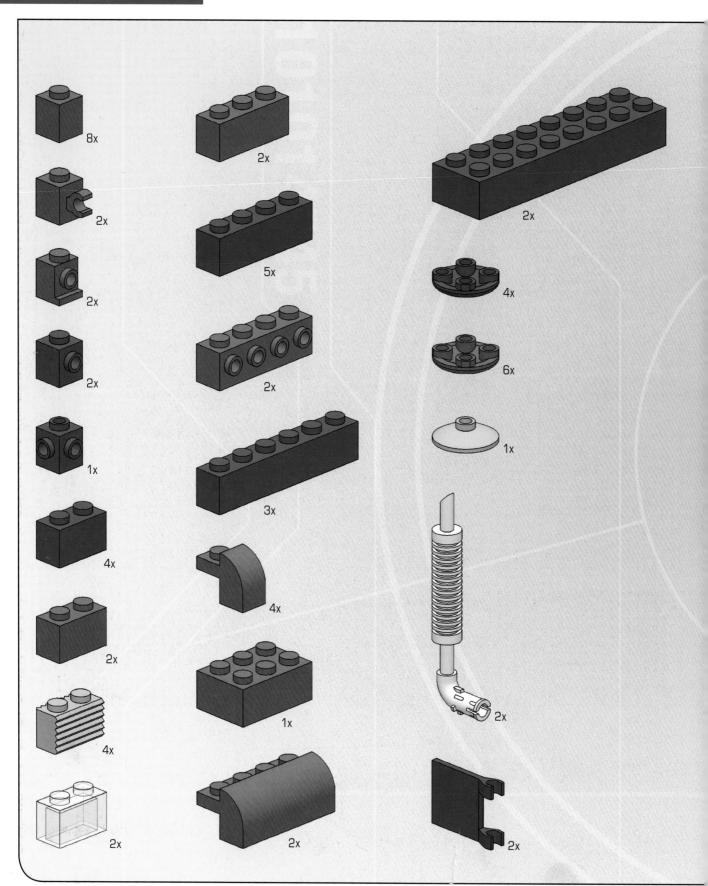

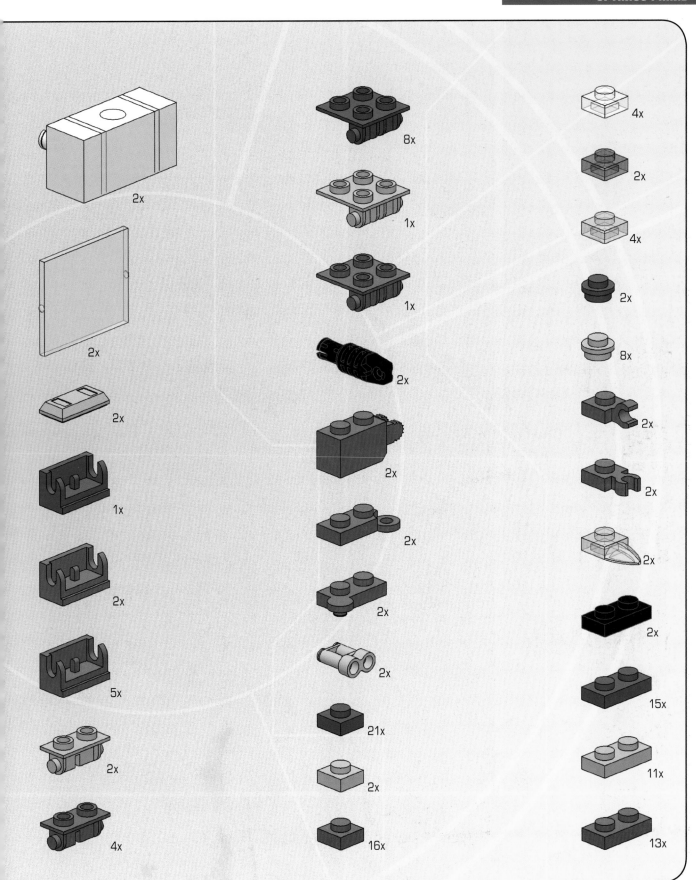

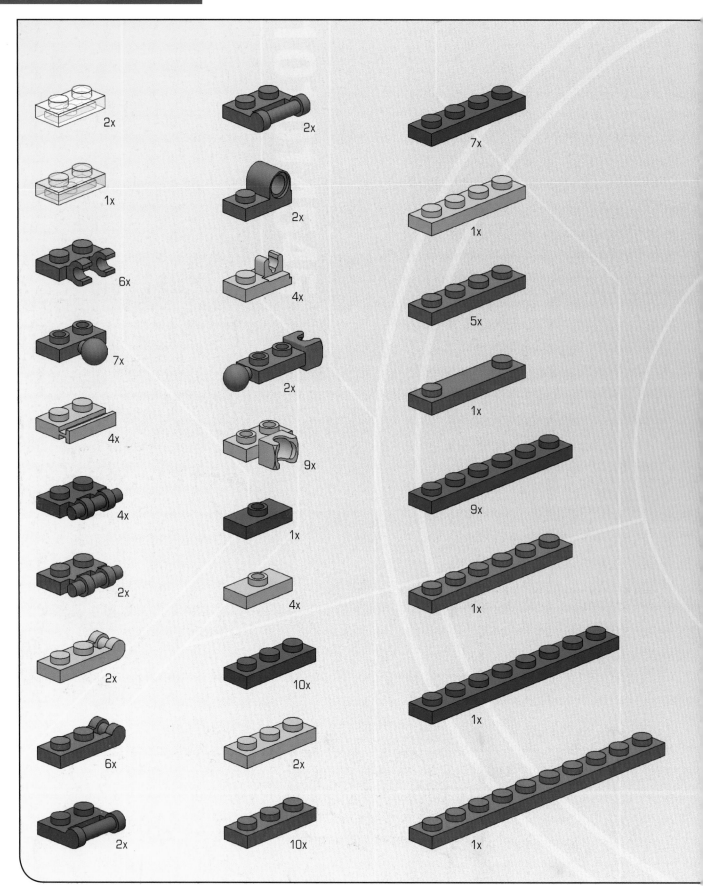

2x

1x

6x

7x

4x

4x

2x

2x

6x

2x

2x

2x

4x

2x

9x

1x

4x

10x

2x

10x

7x

1x

5x

1x

9x

1x

1x

1x

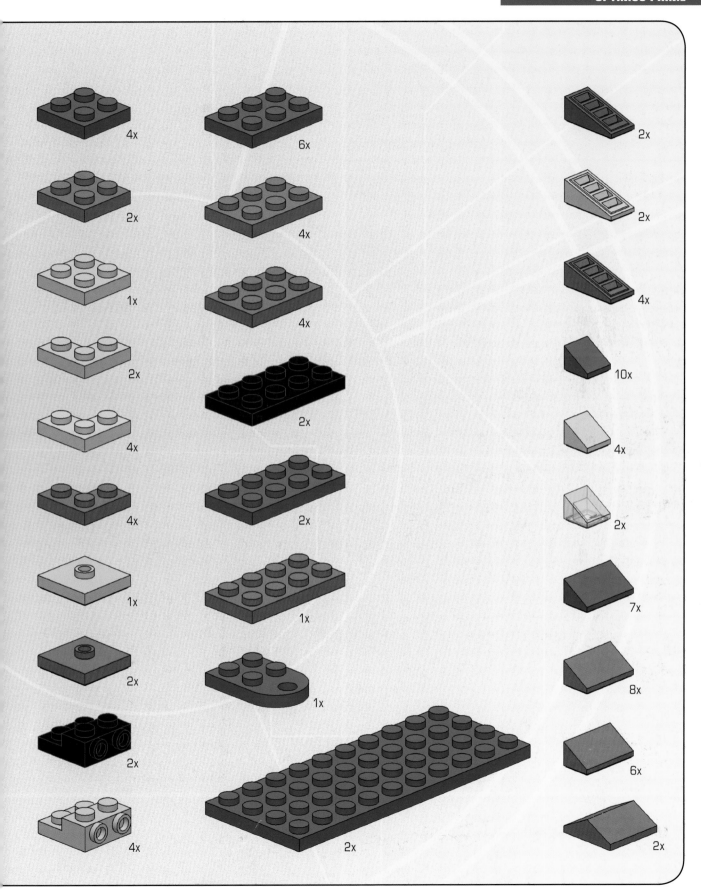

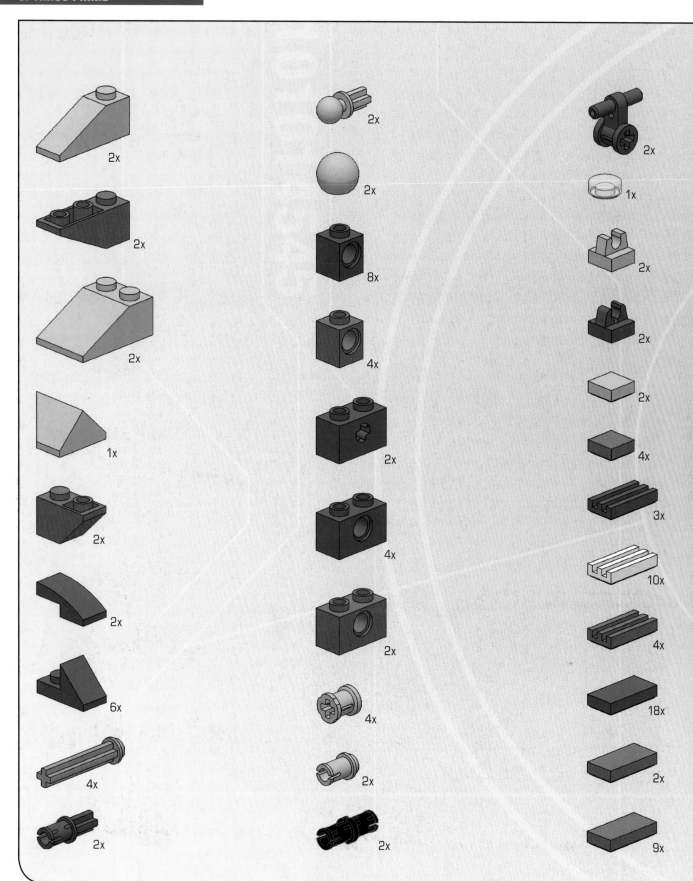

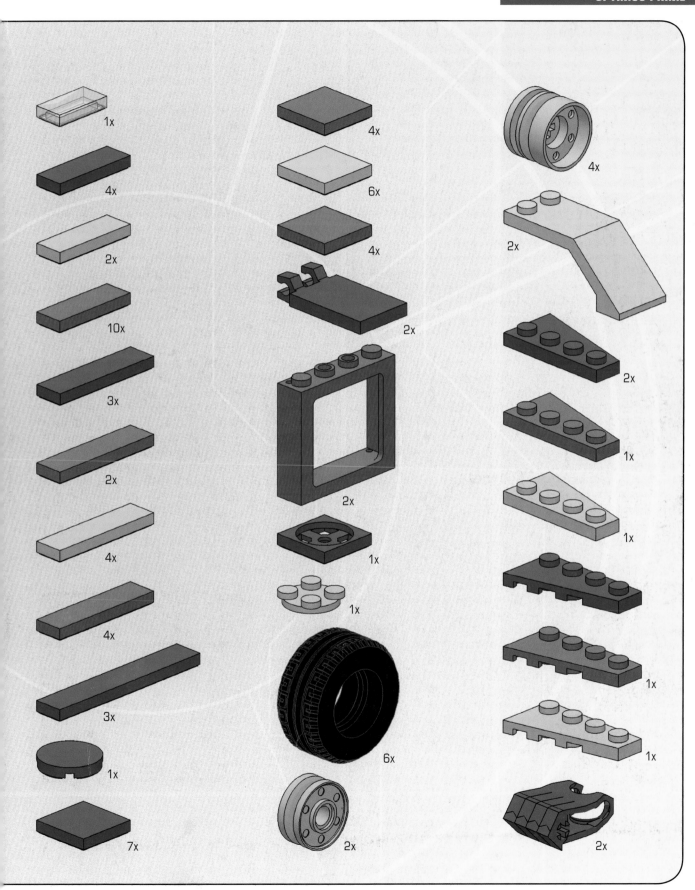

1x

4x

2x

10x

3x

2x

4x

4x

3x

1x

7x

4x

6x

4x

2x

2x

1x

1x

6x

2x

4x

2x

2x

2x

1x

1x

1x

1x

1x

2x